HOW TO BECOME A
Buddha
IN 5 WEEKS

THE SIMPLE WAY TO SELF-REALIZATION

(Come diventare un buddha
in cinque settimane)

by GIULIO CESARE GIACOBBE
translated by Howard Curtis

ARCTURUS

ARCTURUS
Published by Arcturus Canada
A division of Arcturus Publishing Limited
26/27 Bickels Yard
151-153 Bermondsey Street
London SE1 3HA

ISBN-13: 978-1-905555-25-3
ISBN-10: 1-905555-25-3
AD000256EN

British Library Cataloguing-in-Publication Data: a catalogue
record for this book is available from the British Library

This edition printed in 2009

Copyright © 2009 Arcturus Publishing Limited

Printed in China

HOW TO BECOME A
Buddha
IN 5 WEEKS

To my son Yuri
who, as a mortal, was a buddha and who in
dying transmitted his buddha-ness to me, another
mortal, in the year 2558 after the birth of the
Buddha Siddhartha Gautama Sakyamuni

Contents

You, wayfarer in the universe
who go through life like a meteor,
make sure your fall into the void is not in vain
do not go straight from nothing to nothing
but give a meaning to your fleeting presence
in this fleeting reality
cultivating the most sublime of achievements
and the highest goal of Consciousness
which makes Matter great:
love through non-attachment.
A buddha is inside you:
make him grow until you become
another of his incarnations.
In the eternal flow from nothing to nothing
make sure that between one nothing and the other
Consciousness and Love
take their place in the evolution
of this universe.

Introduction

This manual is not about the Buddhist religion.

Its aim is to present the *psychological method* taught originally by the Buddha. (Which means you won't have to shave your head and beg for charity. Best of all, you won't have to dress in orange all the time; quite an advantage if you prefer other colours.)

The sole purpose and objective of this teaching is **liberation from suffering**.

I teach only that which helps us to find the Way. That which is pointless I do not teach. Beyond the fact of whether the universe is finite or infinite, temporary or eternal, there is a truth that must be accepted: the reality of suffering. Suffering comes from causes that can be understood and eliminated. That which I teach helps us to attain detachment, equanimity, peace and liberation. But of that which does not help us to find the Way, I do not speak. [Suttapitaka, Majjhima-Nikaya, Upakkilesa Sutta]

Obviously what is of concern here is not physical suffering, or the Buddha would have gone down in history as a doctor.

Clearly what we are dealing with is *mental* suffering.

In other words, the Buddha was a *psychologist*.[1]
As we can see, mental suffering was already very widespread two thousand five hundred years ago. Indeed, this suffering is traditionally defined as 'the human condition'.

That is exactly what the Buddha's first pronouncement, the First Noble Truth, states: how widespread suffering is.

But what produces suffering?

That is the question that the Buddha asked himself.

The answer he gave was: *a false vision of reality.*

The Buddha proposed an alternative: a vision of reality and a pattern of behaviour capable of giving us serenity, peace, laughter, joy and love.

In other words, well-being and happiness.

Its efficacy has been proved by the widespread dissemination of Buddhism throughout the world.

The form it has assumed is that of a religion, but its aim is *psychological*: the elimination of suffering, and the establishment of a constant state of *serenity*.

In fact, the Buddha's original teaching constitutes, as we shall see, a *psychological method*.

The Buddha's teaching is simple and can be put into practice by anyone.

Even by children.

You are intelligent children and I am certain that you can understand everything I tell you and put it into practice. The Great Way that I have discovered is subtle and profound, but whoever is willing to commit his heart and mind will be in a position to understand it and follow it. [*Suttapitaka, Majjhima-Nikaya, Upakkilesa Sutta*]

Tradition has turned it into a *theory*.[2]

In fact, it is a **practice**.

My teaching is neither a theory nor a philosophy, but the fruit of experience. Everything I say comes from my experience and you too can confirm it through your own experience. Words do not describe reality: only experience shows us its true face. [*Suttapitaka, Majjhima-Nikaya, Upakkilesa Sutta*]

The practice proposed by the Buddha consists of achieving five powers, which we each already possess but simply do not use.

They are: *control of the mind, being in reality, awareness of change, non-attachment* and *universal love*.

We shall see how the achievement of these five powers constitutes the Buddha's original teaching and what you have to do to achieve them.

It takes *five weeks* to achieve them.

One week devoted to each of the five powers.

This is how to use this manual.

First of all, read the whole book in order to obtain an overall idea of the process.

Then reread the chapter devoted to the achievement of the first power and apply yourself to achieving it during the first week.

Then do the same, in the following four weeks, for the remaining four powers.

At the end of the fifth week your buddha-ness will have become *real*, even though you will still only be at an early stage.

You will have become a *buddha*.

From now on, you will only have to *expand* your buddha-ness and *strengthen* it, using my reminders to help you.

The aim of this manual is not only to revive the Buddha's original teaching, which has been forgotten for too long, but also, and above all, to reconstruct that teaching *in a scientific form*, in such a way as to make it comprehensible to everyone and achievable by everyone.

I acknowledge my gratitude to Siddhartha Gautama Sakyamuni who opened the Way and to my son Yuri who, in following it throughout his all too brief life, also led me to it.

Yuri died at the age of twenty-seven: the exact age at which the Buddha attained enlightenment. Yuri was a buddha, one of those incarnations of the Buddha (Bodhisattva) who, according to Buddhism, appear every so often on Earth. From the moment he was born he displayed an incomparable degree of serenity and love. In all his twenty-seven years of life I never once saw him lose his temper or lash out at anyone. On the contrary, he always smiled, was always tolerant towards everyone and communicated to everyone his unconditional love without even speaking, but with a smile and a touch of the hand. You felt his presence inside you. Everyone felt it. Whatever you did, he was always close to you and made you feel his absolute, unconditional love.

He died of nothing more unusual than influenza. But in dying he performed a miracle. He turned his father, this old sinner, into a buddha. He passed his buddha-ness on to me, so that I acquired it through no merit of my own. My life has been transformed. I have seen enlightenment. I have seen and absorbed into my own body, totally and permanently, the absolute precariousness of existence, the one reality of the here and now, and the absolute, exclusive importance of love, laughter and joy. I have seen that it is possible to become a buddha.

My Buddhism is no longer theoretical, it has become real. That is how this book came about. I already knew the Buddha's teaching theoretically but, experiencing that teaching in my own body, I have achieved that buddha-ness which everyone, without having to suffer the loss of a son, can achieve.

NOTES

[1] Jesus, having shown himself to be not only the son of God but also a shrewd *psychologist*, disappointed his earthly father, like all sons, by not following his profession (carpenter) but devoting himself instead to intellectual pursuits (less exhausting but much more dangerous, as was to become clear). It is exciting for psychologists, like me, that out of all possible professions Jesus chose ours. To think that we number the son of God among our members! That our profession now also turns out to include the Buddha is a real stroke of luck! I wouldn't be surprised if Gandhi and Golda Meir were in there somewhere too.

[2] Buddhist philosophy, or rather Buddhist philosophies, have proliferated since the death of the Buddha: according to Dr Edward Conze, one of the greatest scholars of Buddhism, there are fourteen of them, all different.

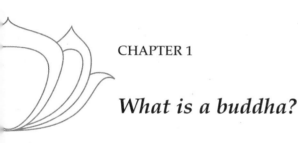

CHAPTER 1

What is a buddha?

What is a buddha?

A buddha isn't a god, a saint, a superman or a super-natural being.[1]

He's one of us.

An ordinary person.

He is simply someone who has eliminated suffering.

Not from the world, of course, but from *within himself.*

He no longer suffers.

He doesn't lose his temper.

He doesn't hate.

He doesn't feel jealousy, envy or resentment.

Or sadness, anxiety or fear.

Or greed, covetousness or selfishness.

But does that mean that he is apathetic, indifferent, without feelings?

Not a bit of it.

He has feelings.

All of them.

But he doesn't exacerbate them.

He doesn't cultivate them.

He doesn't become a slave to them.

He doesn't nourish them.

I am talking about negative feelings.

He nourishes only *positive* feelings.

Feelings of *serenity, peace, laughter, joy, harmony* and *love*.

In other words, he succeeds in remaining serene within himself, nourishing himself on positive feelings, enjoying positive feelings and neutralizing negative feelings.

He is always calm and serene.

His body is always relaxed.

He no longer feels stress or tension.[2]

He lives on joy, laughter, harmony and love.

And he inspires joy, harmony, love, laughter and good humour in those around him.[3]

Because he has attained serenity.

A buddha is someone who has attained serenity and maintains it in every situation.

But how does he do it?

We shall see.

This book has been written to show you.

And to help you become like him.

A buddha.

You will see that it is possible.

It isn't difficult to become a buddha.

You just have to apply yourself.

For the moment all you have to know is that it's possible to become a buddha.

That it's possible for everyone, even you.

Because, as the Buddha said,

Every human being has the nature of a buddha.

In other words, every human being can become a buddha.

Every human being can in fact achieve *buddha-ness*, that is, the ability always to be serene, whatever happens.

But is it really possible?

Yes, of course.

Because, incredible as it may seem,

Our serenity does not depend on situations but on our reaction to them.

The same situation produces different reactions in different people.

And that's not all.

You yourself, in the very same situation, have had different reactions at different times in your life.

Our reaction to situations is in fact *conditioned by our experience*, in other words, by our *past*.

In Eastern culture, this conditioning has been called the *law of karma*.[4]

Karma means 'action'.

This law shows how every one of our actions is conditioned by our *experience*.

In other words, our present is conditioned by our past.

But that also means that *our future is conditioned by our present.*

Therefore, by changing our present, we are in a position to *determine our future.*

If it is true that our reaction to situations is conditioned by our past experience, it is equally true that we are in a position, through *awareness* and *will*, to ensure that our reaction to situations escapes our conditioning and remains *positive*, maintaining our serenity.

This will ensure that our future *will no longer be conditioned in a negative direction* and the maintenance of serenity will become a *spontaneous* pattern of behaviour.

That is how to become a buddha.

The Buddha has in fact been defined precisely as the *non-conditioned*, he who has escaped the conditioning of the past.

We can therefore already, as of now, construct our **serenity**.

We can already, as of now, construct our *personalities as buddhas.*

Of course, this takes *practice*.

But what doesn't take practice?

Has anyone ever learned how to ski, or type, or drive a car, or use a computer without practice?

Everything takes practice.

And why practise to learn how to ski, or type, or drive a car, or use a computer, and not to become a buddha?

Which gives us much more satisfaction, because it makes it possible for us to remain serene in any situation.

The Buddha himself said: you will have to make an *effort*, Right Effort.

But only at first.

Then, with *habit*, it will become spontaneous and natural.

Then you will have become a buddha.

The important thing is that you begin to learn how to neutralize your negative reactions and cultivate your positive reactions.

The important thing is that you start to set in motion the process by which you become a buddha.

Then, with time, you will become an ever more complete buddha.

It is only a matter of time and application.

All you need is one thing: **perseverance**.

If you don't think you have it, there is a trick to obtain it and develop it:

Make your project to become a buddha the centre of your life.

If you do that, your perseverance will bloom like a flower, grow like a tornado, become as solid as a mountain.

If you make your project to become a buddha the centre of your life, you will develop, spontaneously and effortlessly, an invincible perseverance that will lead you to certain success.

21

It's only a question of making an act of will become a *habit*, an act of will that at first will be uncertain and demanding but which then, with practice, will become increasingly easy and spontaneous, until it becomes *automatic*.

The Buddha filled his life with serenity, peace, harmony, good humour, joy and love.

As have many others after him.

That's what you too will be able to do.

They are in fact *mental states.*

And we all have the *power* to achieve and make permanent, or at least frequent, these mental states.

They can be summed up in one word: ***serenity***.

Serenity is the principal characteristic of the Buddha and that is what you will be able to achieve for the *rest of your life* if you follow the instructions in this manual.

You don't have to shave your head and dress in orange or retire to a monastery twelve thousand feet up in the Himalayas.

Although, just like a nice holiday in the mountains, it might help.

As the Dalai Lama has said, the Buddha is inside you whatever you do and wherever you go.[5]

Which means that you can achieve the state of buddha-ness in any place and in any condition.

It is not as impossible as it may seem, or as difficult.

Because your serenity is a *mental state* and your mental states are not only your own business, they depend on you!

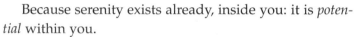

Because serenity exists already, inside you: it is *potential* within you.

In other words, you are already *capable* of achieving it.

You only need to learn how to achieve it *practically*.

I shall explain how to do this in the course of the manual.

Don't think about it now.

The main thing, for now, is that you too can become a buddha.

Let me make one thing clear.

Being a buddha doesn't mean not having friendships and relationships, not forming life plans, not undertaking political, social and professional tasks.

It only means *remaining serene* in every circumstance and *loving other people* (which is indispensable for remaining serene).

Being a buddha means remaining serene in every circumstance and loving other people.

That's all.

I'm sorry if it's not much.

There are buddhas among us.

Many more than you imagine.

The beach of a little fishing village.

The small, squat boats are lined up on the foreshore, the waves of the sea lapping lazily at their broad, colourful hulls.

The old men haul the nets, swollen and alive with fish, from the full bellies of the boats, occasionally exchanging a few words, talking about things they know: fish, the sea, boats, women.

The women move their fingers, expertly and rapidly, between the coils of the lace, and talk among themselves, sometimes in loud, excited voices, sometimes in hushed, secretive tones, sometimes bursting into uproarious laughter that rises into the air like firecrackers exploding.

The children run between the boats, egging one another on with little cries. Some of them are naked.

The cats lying on the doorsteps narrow their eyes in the blinding sun, but keep looking at the nets, overflowing with fish.

The seagulls circle above the beach, looking down at the boats with their sharp eyes and filling the clear, luminous morning air with screeches of protest over the theft of their fish.

He's a young man of twenty-seven.

He has dark blond hair which turns an almost platinum gold in the rays of the sun, and grey-blue eyes which reflect all the depth and luminosity of the sky.

His lips are parted in a vague smile, which greets everything with peace, joy, harmony, acceptance, understanding and love.

It is as if with his eyes and his smile he is embracing this little corner of the world – the beach, the boats, the nets, the old men, the women, the children, the cats, the seagulls – caressing them with infinite tenderness and gentleness.

Time runs in its deep riverbed, but the young man is at every point along its banks, in every cliff, in every beach, in every stone, in every bush.

He is at every point of the river of life and the universe.

This little corner of the world becomes the whole world, gathers the whole universe, and the boats, the nets, the old men, the women, the children, the cats, the seagulls become all the living beings – men, women, animals, plants – and all the things – the stones, the clouds, the stars – that the universe has poured into the river of time and submerged in its warm and foamy, then cold and still, waters.

The young man looks and smiles.

His look, like his smile, is older than the boats, the nets, the old men, the women, the children, the cats, the seagulls.

In his look and in his smile there is the silence of peace, joy, harmony, acceptance, understanding and universal love.

NOTES

[1] The Buddha is not considered a deity, even in the Buddhist religion, which sees him as an advocate of liberation from the slavery of rebirths.

[2] The only problem with becoming a buddha is that you put on a little weight, since, being without stress, your muscles no longer contract with nervous tension (it is no coincidence that the Buddha is always depicted as being somewhat plump). But when you have become a buddha, you stop caring about your figure.

[3] Humour is another characteristic that is acquired, or gets stronger, when you become a buddha. The hilarity of Tibetan monks, the humour of Zen monks, is famous. It derives from their condition of relaxation and serenity, which allows them not only to see the funny side of life and laugh about it, but also to *create* hilarity as a positive mental state. As everyone knows, 'laughter is the best medicine'.

[4] The law of *karma* was discovered by Eastern culture in very ancient times (even before the Buddha); after the advent of writing it was described in the *Bhagavad Gita*, a work that forms part of the Indian epic poem *The Mahabharata*, dating from the 5th century BC, and in the classic treatise on Yoga, the *Yoga Sutra*, from the 3rd century BC. In Western culture the law of karma was only discovered in the 20th century by Sigmund Freud, who identified the conditioning of the memory of the past (the unconscious) over the present as the cause of *neurosis*.

[5] I don't know where and when he said it but, given the Buddha's pot belly, he must have said it somewhere!

CHAPTER 2

Who was the Buddha?

Siddhartha Gautama Sakyamuni, known as 'the Buddha' (the Awakened One), was a real character in history.

He was born in 563 BC in Kapilavatthu, capital of the kingdom of the Sakyas, of which his father Suddhodana was the monarch, in a region of the Himalayas close to what is now Nepal.

According to tradition, his mother Mahamaya, who gave him the name *Siddhartha*, died eight days after he was born, and he was brought up by her sister Pajapati Gotami, the king's second wife, from whom he took his second name.[1]

From the Sakyas, the tribe to which he belonged, he took his third name.

According to legend, his father, King Suddhodana, received a prophecy that his first-born son (Siddhartha) would abandon the kingdom and renounce all claim to the throne.

To ward off this possibility, which he considered a great calamity, he kept Siddhartha confined within the royal palace, forbidding him any contact with the outside world. (Siddhartha had a brother, but clearly, in India as elsewhere, second sons were considered less than nothing. In the West, they had to invent the Crusades for themselves, in order to have something to do.)

Siddhartha had a carefree childhood and youth.

When he was twenty, a marriage was arranged for him with his cousin, Princess Yasodhara, the daughter of King Dandapani of the kingdom of the Koliyas and of King Suddhodana's sister, Queen Pamita.

At twenty-two, immediately after the birth of his son Rahula, Siddhartha discovered the suffering present in the outside world, of which he had been unaware until then. He abandoned his family, the royal palace and his position and went in search of the Way that leads to liberation. (Like all great men [and all adults] he behaved, as we see, like a real bastard. But perhaps he only did it to demonstrate that prophecies work.)

For five years, he wandered the kingdom in search of masters and practised the form of asceticism traditional in Indian culture, Yoga.

He first became a disciple of the ascetic Alara Kalama, then of the ascetic Uddaka Ramaputta, and under their guidance experienced ever deeper states of *trance*, in which suffering is transcended.

He realized, however, that this liberation from suffering was limited to the state of *trance* and was therefore not permanent.

Then, for six months, he practised the most extreme form of asceticism, mortification of the body, until he realized that not even that way led to permanent liberation from suffering.[2]

He then devoted himself to observing his own sensations, his own emotions, his own thoughts, through an awareness of the phenomena that present themselves to the consciousness. (Clearly, he invented psychoanalysis.)

He saw that they are constantly being born and constantly dying, in a continuous state of becoming, and in this way discovered that the true nature of reality is *constant transformation*. This is the *panta rhei* of Heraclitus' philosophy.

This was his first discovery.

The second was that no one thing can exist without the existence of all the others, but that all are linked among themselves in a universal network of interdependence or mutual causation. (This is the principle discovered recently in physics and known as the *butterfly effect*.)

Sitting under a pipal tree, in a forest near the village of Uruvela, Siddhartha deepened his analysis of reality.[3]

He was brought food by two young people: Svasti, a very poor orphan who watched the buffalo, and Sujata, the daughter of the head of the village.[4]

One day, after Svasti had left him to take the buffalo home, Siddhartha was filled with the sensation that that night he would attain the Great Awakening.

Thanks to awareness, his mind, body and breathing were perfectly united.

The practice of mental presence had made him capable of developing a great power of concentration, which he was now able to use to flood his body and mind with awareness.

Unwaveringly, Siddhartha flooded his own mind with awareness.

He saw that human beings suffer because they do not understand that they share the same nature as all creatures: ignorance gives rise to myriad sorrows, confusions and difficulties; greed, anger, arrogance, doubt, jealousy and fear are all rooted in ignorance.

Learning to calm his mind in order to see deeper into the true nature of things, Siddhartha attained the overall understanding that dissolves every anxiety and every pain, replacing them with acceptance and love.

He saw that understanding and love are one and the same: without understanding there can be no love and without love there can be no right action.

He saw that in order to develop clear understanding it is necessary to live in mental presence, in direct contact with life in the here and now, seeing with awareness what really happens both inside and outside us.

Mental presence and awareness lead to permanent liberation from suffering.

Siddhartha realized that he had found the Great Way.

It was not an intellectual way but a way of experience, not a theoretical way but a practical one.

Bringing him his food the following day, Sujata saw him looking radiant.

A hundred times she had seen him sitting under the pipal tree in dignity and majesty, but today there was something different about him.

As she looked at him, Sujata felt her own woes and anxieties vanish.

A joy as fresh as the spring breeze filled her heart.

She felt that she desired nothing more than what she had, that everything in the universe was good and benevolent and that nobody had to fear or despair any longer.

She took a few steps and placed the food in front of him.

Then she bowed, feeling that the peace and joy permeating Siddhartha was also being transmitted to her.

'Sit down beside me,' said Siddhartha with a smile. 'I thank you for the food and water you have brought me all these months. Today is the happiest day of my life because last night I found the Great Way. Share this happiness with me. Soon I will teach the Way to everyone.'

Sujata put her hands together and asked permission to speak. 'You are the awakened one, he who shows us how to live in awareness. May we call you "the Awakened One?"'

Siddhartha nodded. 'That would make me very happy.'

Sujata's eyes shone. 'In the Magadhi language,' she said, 'the word *budh* means "to wake up". A person who has woken up is therefore a *buddha*. May we call you "the Buddha?"'

Siddhartha nodded again.

He was twenty-seven years old.

The Buddha devoted the rest of his life to spreading his discoveries so that other human beings could achieve enlightenment and liberation from suffering.

Travelling all over his kingdom and then descending the Ganges to the neighbouring kingdoms of the Koliyas, the Mallas, the Kosalas, the Licchavis, the Angas, the Magadhas, the Kasis and the Vatsas, he converted thousands of people, founding communities (*sangha*) of monks (*bhikkhu*), to whom he set out in a series of sermons (*sutta*) his discipline, the *dharma*.

As a magnificent example of universal love, at the insistence of Queen Pajapati, his adoptive mother, who was clearly not at all happy with her marriage, he let her found a female *sangha*, with herself, obviously, at its head.

At the age of seventy-two, in 491 BC, after a schism within the *sangha* led by his disciple Devadatta, two attempts on his life (in the second of which he was wounded), and a serious illness from which he recovered, the Buddha himself announced, three months in advance, his own death, which occurred in a forest near Kusinara, a village in the kingdom of the Mallas neighbouring his own native land. (This ability to announce one's own death in advance is characteristic of the enlightened or initiated. Which doesn't rule out the possibility that some of them kill themselves in order to prove they were right.)

After six days and six nights of ceremonies, with offerings of flowers, the burning of incense, and music and dancing, in which not only the *bhikkhu* took part, but also the inhabitants of Kusinara and the nearby town of Pava, the Buddha's body was transported to Pava for the funeral. It was wrapped in cloth, placed in an iron coffin, lifted on to a large pyre of scented wood and cremated in the presence of hundreds of people.

His ashes were divided and placed inside eight *stupas* (funerary monuments) at Kusinara and Pava in the kingdom of the Mallas, Kapilavatthu in the kingdom of the Sakyas, Rajagaha in the kingdom of the Magadhas, Vesali in the kingdom of the Licchavis, Allakappa in the kingdom of the Bulis, Ramagama in the kingdom of the Koliyas and Vethadipa in the kingdom of the Vethas.[5]

NOTES

[1] As with many great men, myths concerning the birth of the Buddha have proliferated in the popular imagination. According to one of these myths, the Buddha's mother, who after thirty-two months of marriage was still a virgin (*it is the destiny of the mothers of great men to remain inescapably, and incredibly, virgins even when they become pregnant*), dreamed of a beautiful white elephant who entered her right side. Ten months later (*as is well known, elephants have a somewhat longer pregnancy than ours*), as she was travelling to her ancestral home, she went into labour and gave birth, standing up and holding a branch of a fig tree (*a notoriously treacherous tree*).

[2] It is this period that gives rise to the iconography that depicts the Buddha as thin and emaciated. As we shall see, the suffering (and the thinness) of the Buddha is temporary and does not represent his true personality. In the Buddha there is no room for suffering, since its elimination is the purpose of all his teaching. The true dimension of the Buddha is pleasure.

[3] What on earth is a pipal tree? I am launching a competition among my readers to see who can solve this mystery. The winners will get a crash course on how to attain enlightenment.

[4] This business of being a parasite on others is the one characteristic of the Buddha (who never worked a day in his life) that I urge you not to imitate. Not because there is anything bad about begging. But there is something a bit *too* Eastern about this way, which tends towards *passivity*. I propose a *Western* way to Buddhism, an *active* way that allows you to create, construct and compete as you would in normal life. But without stress. Which also means more efficiently.

[5] A brief biography based on the work of Thich Nhat Hanh, *Old Path White Clouds*, published in 2003 by Full Circle Publishing Ltd.

CHAPTER 3

The Buddha's original teaching

To infer the Buddha's original teaching from the vast array of Buddhist literature is no easy task.[1]

There are three principal canons (traditions): the Pali, the Chinese and the Tibetan, each in their respective languages.

The Pali canon is the oldest, which should make it the most reliable.[2]

But it too was written a long time – more than two centuries – after Siddhartha's death.[3]

It is therefore likely that the speeches attributed to the Buddha were partly reworked, partly invented.

They are collected in the *Suttapitaka*, one of the three parts into which the Pali canon – which is actually known as *Tripitaka* ('three baskets') – is divided.[4]

The three canons are different from each other and attribute different pronouncements to the Buddha.

But there are two pronouncements that are quoted in all the canons: the **Four Noble Truths** and the **Noble Eightfold Path**.

The Four Noble Truths

Brothers, there are four truths: the existence of suffering, the cause of suffering, the elimination of suffering and the way that leads to the elimination of suffering. I call them the Four Noble Truths.

Brothers, the First Noble Truth is the existence of suffering.

Birth, old age, illness and death are suffering.

Sadness, anger, envy, fear, anxiety and despair are suffering.

The absence of what we love is suffering.

The presence of what we hate is suffering.

Desire is suffering.

Aversion is suffering.

This is the First Noble Truth.

Brothers, the Second Noble Truth is the cause of suffering.

The cause of suffering is attachment.

Attachment in its turn is caused by ignorance.

The ignorance that causes attachment is ignorance of reality, it is ignorance of the fact that reality is impermanent.

Ignorance of reality produces attachment because we take that which is impermanent as being permanent.

Attachment produces sadness, anger, envy, fear, anxiety and despair.

This is the Second Noble Truth.

Brothers, the Third Noble Truth is the extinction of suffering.

Suffering can only be extinguished with the extinction of its cause, that is, ignorance and therefore attachment.

This is the Third Noble Truth.

Brothers, the Fourth Noble Truth is the way that leads to the extinction of suffering: that is the Noble Eightfold Path.

This is the Fourth Noble Truth. [*Suttapitaka, Majjhima-Nikaya, Saccavibhanga Sutta*]

THE NOBLE EIGHTFOLD PATH

Brothers, the Noble Eightfold Path of Right Understanding, Right Thought, Right Speech, Right Action, Right Livelihood, Right Effort, Right Mindfulness and Right Concentration is what I call the Right Paths.[5]

By following the Noble Eightfold Path I have attained understanding, liberation and peace.

Brothers, why do I call these paths the Right Paths?

I call them right because they do not deny suffering but indicate in the direct experience of suffering the way to overcome it.

The Noble Eightfold Path is the way of awareness, based on Right Mindfulness.

By practising Right Mindfulness we develop Right Concentration, which allows us to attain Right Understanding.

Through Right Concentration we achieve Right Understanding, Right Thought, Right Speech, Right Action, Right Livelihood and Right Effort.

The awareness that develops from these liberates us from the shackles of suffering and gives birth to true peace and true joy. [*Suttapitaka, Majjhima-Nikaya, Pasarasi Sutta*]

The Four Noble Truths and the Noble Eightfold Path constitute the heart of the ***Buddha's original teaching*** .

But do not think that the Four Noble Truths and the Noble Eightfold Path are not enough to construct something like Buddhism.

They are important and demanding prescriptions for *psychological* and *behavioural attitudes*.

And they are more than enough.

Naturally with a few refinements which we can also find in Buddhist literature.

Since the Four Noble Truths and the Noble Eightfold Path constitute the essence of Buddhism and describe the practice to which we must apply ourselves in order to achieve buddha-ness, it is necessary to clarify and analyse what they consist of.

I'll begin by examining the Four Noble Truths.

NOTES

[1] 'The quantity of Buddhist scripture is truly vast, and covers tens of thousands of pages. The Pali canon, which is limited to a single sect, fills 45 huge volumes in the complete Thai edition, excluding commentaries. The Chinese and Tibetan canons, on the other hand, include the work of all the schools that left their mark on China and Tibet. In the most recent Japanese edition, the Chinese Scriptures consist of 100 volumes of 1,000 pages in tiny print, while the Tibetan Scriptures take up 325 volumes.' [E. Conze, editor, *Buddhist Scriptures*, Penguin Classics, 1959]

[2] Pali (a popular version of Sanskrit) was the spoken language in the region where the Buddha lived, and was therefore the language he himself used. I will take this canon, insofar as it is universally acknowledged as the most reliable, as the source of all my quotations.

[3] Between the second and the third councils of the Buddhist community, held at Vesali in 340 BC and Pataliputta in 246 BC respectively.

[4] The other two parts are the *Vinayapitaka*, concerning the rules of conduct of the monks, and the *Abhidhammapitaka*, which expounds the theoretical basis of the doctrine.

[5] The terms used in the definitions of the Noble Eightfold Path differ in the three principal traditions, and therefore in the three canons, as well as in the various Western traditions. Those quoted here are the ones used in the already cited work *Old Path White Clouds* by Thich Nhat Hanh, since that is easily available to the Western reader.

CHAPTER 4

The Four Noble Truths

The Four Noble Truths are about *suffering*.

They are pronouncements concerning: **1** the existence of suffering; **2** its cause; **3** the means to eliminate it; **4** the way that leads to its elimination. In more detail:

1
the existence of suffering
**OBSERVATION OF THE WIDESPREAD
EXISTENCE OF SUFFERING**

2
the cause of suffering
**IDENTIFICATION OF THE CAUSE OF SUFFERING:
IGNORANCE OF THE IMPERMANENT NATURE
OF REALITY**

3
the elimination of suffering
**INDICATION OF THE MEANS TO ELIMINATE SUFFERING:
AWARENESS OF THE IMPERMANENT NATURE
OF REALITY**

4

the way that leads to the elimination of suffering
**PROCEDURE FOR ELIMINATING SUFFERING:
PRACTICE OF THE NOBLE EIGHTFOLD PATH**

The Four Noble Truths constitute the *basis* of Buddhism.

They state that suffering is very widespread, that it is due to a false vision of reality, that it can be eliminated by means of a correct vision of reality, and that this vision can be achieved and maintained through the practice of the Noble Eightfold Path.

Since the suffering to which the Buddha refers is a systematic, permanent suffering, it is understood that this is a *neurotic suffering.*

Indeed, according to Buddhist psychology, the structure of the Ego – in other words, the normal structure of the human personality – is a *neurotic* structure.[1]

This apparently paradoxical statement can be demonstrated both theoretically and experientially.

Theoretically, it refers to the mental structure of a personality attracted to, and absorbed in, the symbolic expansion of the *Ego* and the abnormal development of *thought*.

Since man began his mental evolution, which has made thought his main perceptual activity, his *Ego* – that is, the image the human being has of himself – has gone past the natural limits of his body.

Our Ego has spread to our material possessions, to our financial status, to our emotional ties (and therefore to other living creatures), as well as to our social roles, our mental states, our patterns of behaviour – the stereotyped images of our culture.

In other words, *conceptual symbols*.

Nowadays we identify not only with our bodies, but also with our houses, our cars, our TVs, our bank accounts, our families, our friends, our professions, our prestige, our social roles.

According to Buddhist psychology, this is the root cause of neurosis and therefore of human suffering.

It is a neurotic process, in so far as it is a process of estrangement from reality – in other words, from the natural correspondence between the *Ego* and the body.

In neurosis, the *Ego* identifies with an ever increasing, ever more complex series of *mental symbols* based on values that are *social* or *cultural* rather than natural.

Suffering clearly derives from an expansion of the Ego's state of vulnerability, which increases with the increase in the number of objects with which it identifies.

Experientially, the recurring state of human mental suffering can be clearly observed.

Nowadays, with the advent of a consumer culture based not only on possession and on social status, which has always existed in human history, but also on the ability to produce and consume, the situation has undoubtedly got worse: the widespread existence of neurosis and consequently of mental suffering is evident all around us.[2]

The state of buddha-ness is simply the natural state of non-neurosis.

That explains why *buddha-ness* can be achieved by anyone, as the Buddha declared: because it is not an exceptional, superhuman state, but simply the *natural state*, which, as it is not very widespread, is commonly considered *exceptional*.[3]

The state of buddha-ness can be achieved by following the Noble Eightfold Path.

Let us examine the elements of this Path, one by one.

NOTES

[1] 'We can begin by discussing the origin of all psychological problems, the origin of the neurotic mind. It is a tendency to identify with desires and conflicts connected with the outside world. And the first question to be asked is whether these conflicts really exist in the outside world or if they are in fact inner conflicts.' [Chôgyam Trungpa, *Glimpses of Abhidharma*, 1975]

[2] What makes us neurotic is not so much the excitable life we lead as the *mental attitude* we adopt towards it: as if our happiness really depended on success. This produces *stress*, which is the exact opposite of *serenity*. Happiness is essentially serenity, and therefore serenity, not success, is the true gauge of our happiness. The state of buddha-ness allows us to achieve genuine serenity, without giving up on the idea of success.

[3] 'We are not normal and natural. We are absolutely abnormal, we are sick, we are mad! It is just that, since everyone is like us, we do not realize it: madness is so normal that not being mad seems abnormal. The Buddha is abnormal.' (Osho Reineesh, *Tantra, Spirituality and Sex*, 1984)

CHAPTER 5

Right Understanding

He smiled and looked up at a leaf of the pipal tree standing out against the blue sky, the tip of which was fluttering towards him as if calling him.

Observing it in depth, Gautama clearly distinguished in it the presence of the sun and the stars, because without the sun and the stars that leaf would never have existed.

And he saw the earth, time, space: all present in the leaf.

In truth, at that precise moment, the whole universe was manifest in the leaf.

The reality of the leaf was an astounding miracle.

He saw that it is the existence of all things that makes the existence of each thing possible.

The one contains the whole and the whole is contained in the one.

The leaf and his body were one and the same.

Neither of the two possessed a permanent and separate self, neither of the two could exist independently of the rest of the universe.

Seeing the interdependent nature of all things, Siddhartha therefore also saw their empty nature: all things are empty of a separate and isolated self.

He realized that the key to liberation lies in the two principles of interdependence and non-self.

Illuminating the rivers of perception, Siddhartha understood that impermanence and the absence of a self are the conditions that are indispensable to life.

Without impermanence, without the lack of a self, nothing would be able to grow and evolve.

If a grain of rice did not have the nature of impermanence and of non-self, it would not be able to turn into a seedling.

If the clouds were not impermanent and devoid of a self, they would not be able to change to rain.

If his nature were not impermanent and devoid of a self, a child would not be able to turn into an adult.

Therefore accepting life means accepting impermanence and the absence of a self.

The cause of suffering is the false notion of permanence and of a separate self.

Seeing this, Siddhartha attained the understanding that there is neither birth nor death, neither creation nor destruction, neither one nor many, neither inside nor outside, neither large nor small, neither pure nor impure.

All are false distinctions created by the intellect.

When we penetrate the empty nature of things, mental barriers are overcome and we are liberated from the cycle of suffering.[1]

Right Understanding has been handed down by Buddhist tradition under the name of *enlightenment*.

But what, in concrete terms, is Right Understanding?

Clearly, it is the *understanding of the true nature of reality*.

For the sake of clarity, it may be more correct to say that Right Understanding is *knowledge* of the true nature of reality.

Ignorance of reality – the exact opposite of knowledge – is what the Buddha considers the cause of suffering:

> *Brothers, the cause of suffering is ignorance. Because of ignorance, men do not see the reality of life and allow themselves to be imprisoned in the flames of desire, anger, envy, anxiety, fear and despair.* [Suttapitaka, Samyutta-Nikaya, Dhammacakkapavattana Sutta]

It may therefore be more correct if it is called **right knowledge .**

Right knowledge, then, consists of a correct knowledge of reality, undistorted by ignorance.

But what is *reality*?

The definition traditionally attributed to the Buddha is quite clear.

Reality is *constant change.*

Reality is constant change.

In other words, reality is, as the Buddha says, *impermanent.*

All our experience demonstrates that the things and people around us change constantly and we ourselves change constantly.

Situations change constantly.

Our bodies change constantly.

Our minds change constantly.

The universe around us changes constantly.

But the Buddha's discovery did not stop there.

He also discovered that *the existence of each thing is conditioned by the existence of all the others*.

Each thing is conditioned by all the others.

This truth, too, is demonstrated by our experience.

Could an animal exist without the animals that have given birth to it and without all the animals that have preceded it in evolution?

Could animals exist without the plants that feed them?

Could plants exist without water and sunlight?

Could our planet and our sun exist without the rest of the universe?

Could you exist without the universe?

Consider also the beautiful idea that this universe could not exist without you.[2]

In fact it would not be *this* universe.

You are necessary to the existence of this universe, just as this universe is necessary to your existence.

Because every thing is connected with every other thing.

Nothing can exist *independently of all the rest.*

This is the meaning of the expression 'empty of a self' or 'non-self': no one thing is capable of existing *in and of itself*; that is, alone, without the rest of the universe.

As we have seen, the discovery that reality is made up of things in a state of constant transformation and that all things are connected with each other constitutes the famous *enlightenment.*

Right knowledge, then, leads to **enlightenment**.

The Buddha's famous **enlightenment** *is simply Right Understanding or Knowledge.*

Siddhartha considered the discovery of the true nature of reality so important and pivotal as to constitute a genuine *enlightenment*, an event that led him to define himself as the Buddha, the enlightened one.

Why?

Obviously, it is not knowledge of the truth in itself that is so important.

We know that what interested the Buddha was not knowledge but liberation from suffering.

A *practical* interest.

All right, I have grasped that reality is made up of things in a state of constant transformation and all connected with each other.

But what then?

What am I to do with this discovery?

What conclusion do I draw from it?

The conclusion I draw is this: that if everything is in a state of constant transformation, *I cannot become attached to anything.*

We cannot become attached to anything.

Because nothing that exists is immutable, nothing remains the same all the time.

Thinking it does is an *illusion*.

Therefore we are obliged, from existential evidence and for the sake of mental consistency, to develop **non-attachment**.

Non-attachment is the psychological key that opens the door to liberation from suffering.

Non-attachment *leads to liberation from suffering.*

It is obvious, in fact, that if I no longer become attached to anything, all my worries, my problems, my anxieties, my fears – in other words, my mental suffering – will melt away like snow in the sun.

Because suffering derives from *attachment to a situation different from what in fact is*: from a desire for something I don't have or from an aversion to something I do have.

As the Buddhist tradition puts it, suffering *derives either from separation from what we love or union with what we hate.*

Non-attachment therefore fulfils the initial task to which the Buddha applied himself: eliminating suffering.

To put it more fully:

Right Knowledge **(enlightenment)** *consists of*
the awareness that **things** and **people change**
constantly *and are* **all connected with each other**
and therefore to the development of **non-attachment.**

This first precept, non-attachment, would be enough to
achieve the Buddhism preached by the Buddha and eliminate mental suffering from our life.

It is obvious that this is a *psychological* precept, in so
far as it prescribes a specific *mental attitude:* seeing reality
for what it is.

But the Buddha, as the shrewd psychologist that he
was, realized that the average person finds it difficult to
gain and maintain awareness of the impermanence of
reality and to behave and act accordingly.

The average person needs to know how to behave and
act in concrete terms, in order to maintain that awareness
and make it effective.

That is where the other seven elements of the Noble
Eightfold Path come in.

NOTES

[1] *Buddhacarita*, III, 22 (a poem probably written in the first half of the
1st century AD by Ashvaghosa).
[2] That is what I always say to patients suffering depression. It gives
them momentary relief, but then they fall back into the one thought that
obsesses them: that the universe has been created with the sole aim of
cheating them.

CHAPTER 6

Right Thought

Brothers, practise Right Thought.

Right Thought consists of thought in which there is neither confusion nor distraction, neither anger nor hate, neither desire nor lust. [Vinayapitaka, Vibhanga Sutta]

Brothers, Right Thought consists of thought in which there is universal love. [Suttapitaka, Majjhima-Nikaya, Piyajatika Sutta]

But what is Right Thought in concrete terms?

Obviously, a thought in which there is no *suffering*.

And what constitutes suffering, in our thought?

As the Buddha said: *confusion, distraction, anger, hate, desire and lust.*

We need to eliminate them.

But how?

Brothers, confusion and distraction, anger and hate, desire and lust can be overcome by practising the Four Contemplations.

To overcome confusion and distraction, practise the contemplation of breathing: it will clear your mind and increase the power of your concentration.

To overcome anger and hate, practise the contemplation of compassion: it will throw light on the causes of the anger and hate present in your mind and in the minds of those who have aroused them in you.

To overcome desire, practise the contemplation of impermanence: it will throw light on the beginning and end of all things.

To overcome lust, practise the contemplation of death: it will throw light on the decay of all things. [Vinayapitaka, Vibhanga Sutta]

Confusion, distraction, anger, hate, desire and lust obviously constitute *negative thought.*

But it is not enough to eliminate negative thought.

We must also construct *positive thought.*

What are positive thoughts?

Loving kindness, compassion, shared joy and non-attachment are wonderful, profound mental states.

I call them the Four Incommensurables.

By practising them, you will become a source of vitality and happiness for all creatures. [Suttapitaka, Majjhima-Nikaya, Cularahulovada Sutta]

In a word, *positive thought.*

Right Thought therefore consists of the systematic elimination of negative thought and the systematic construction of positive thought.

Right Thought consists of the elimination of negative thought and the construction of positive thought.

CHAPTER 7

Right Speech, Right Action, Right Livelihood

Right Speech, Right Action and Right Livelihood consist of not doing violence to any living creature, either to others or to ourselves, in thought, word or deed. [*Vinayapitaka, Mahavagga Sutta*]

As we can see, Right Speech, Right Action and Right Livelihood are *moral precepts* rather than strictly psychological procedures.

They find expression in the Buddhist tradition in the *Five Precepts*.

My disciples make an effort to live simply and in consciousness and undertake to apply the Five Precepts, which are: do not kill, do not steal, do not commit violent acts, speak the truth and abstain from taking substances that obscure the mind. [*Vinayapitaka, Mahavagga Sutta*]

The Five Precepts are rules of conduct that aim to place us in a position not to generate suffering, but are not enough in themselves to liberate us from neurotic suffering once it has been established.

Therefore, we can leave them out of our method for achieving buddha-ness.

But it might be useful to clarify something.

What is Right Livelihood?

Simply, the *profession* we practise in order to make a living.

Without claiming that we should all become monks, it is necessary, according to Buddhist tradition, to exercise a profession that does not lead us to violate the Five Precepts.

For example, hired killers, drug dealers and arms traffickers cannot attain a state of buddha-ness.

Not because these professions are *immoral*.

Buddhism does not deal with questions of morality.

But because the *sense of guilt*, however unconscious, that may derive from the exercise of these professions is a cause of mental suffering that cannot be eliminated even with the practice of Buddhism, in so far as it is constantly renewed by the exercise of the profession.

In fact, devoting ourselves to a profession that causes suffering to other people eventually gives rise to suffering in us, too, precisely because it produces in us a *sense of guilt*.

It is necessary, therefore, to practise a profession that does not cause suffering either to ourselves or to others.

It is obvious that a sense of guilt depends on the morality with which we have been brought up.

In Buddhism there is no moral imperative of the Kantian type, which states that moral good is a value in itself (a typically Western notion).

Instead, an *instrumental* value is ascribed to morality.

This does not mean that it is any less categorical.

In fact, it is essential for mental well-being and therefore survival.

In other words, it is necessary to do good, or rather not to do bad (that is, not to cause suffering to living creatures), not because this is an absolute good in itself, but because causing suffering to living creatures creates in us a *sense of guilt* that becomes a cause of suffering to ourselves.

Unlike the Western tradition, this approach to morality, which is strictly speaking *psychological*, takes the historical and cultural dimension of morality into account.

For an Amazon headhunter, for example, decapitating an enemy, shrinking his head and sticking it on his belt is an act of great social merit and does not produce any sense of guilt.[1]

The same thing has happened, and still happens, to soldiers in every period and in every country when they kill other human beings in the name of the most diverse ideals and social interests.

The expression 'to do evil', and therefore to suffer from a sense of guilt, ultimately assumes a meaning only in relation to the accepted morality of the society in which we have been brought up.

The important thing is to eliminate the more or less unconscious causes of the sense of guilt, and therefore of mental suffering. We cannot do this through the practice of Buddhism, but through avoiding a way of life that is contrary to the morality in which we have been brought up.

The moral rules handed down by the Buddhist tradition are the moral rules common to almost all human cultures,[2] which is why the Buddha was able to adopt them as absolute.

It is necessary, however, to make one thing clear.

Although it is true that these moral rules are not really part of the psychological method taught by the Buddha, they cannot be excluded from our project to achieve and maintain the state of buddha-ness.

In fact, having adopted, even if only instrumentally, the moral protocol as absolute, it becomes binding.

That is why I have included universal love among the five powers of buddha-ness: without it, the state of buddha-ness cannot be either achieved or maintained.

Not causing suffering to others is a categorical imperative that cannot be separated from the commitment not to generate suffering within oneself.

To give a practical example, a buddha would never cheat on his or her spouse, even if their relationship was bad, because this would cause suffering to the person who was being cheated on.

If the marital relationship were really a source of suffering for everyone, it would be better to bring it to an end.

But if only he or she were suffering, a buddha would work to eliminate the suffering inside himself or herself and not abandon the family, because even this would cause others the suffering he or she has undertaken to eliminate.

This makes Buddhism the bringer of a morality that had never been seen in the history of humanity up until that point, and which would then find a fuller expression in Christianity.

That is why it not only assumed spontaneously the form of a religion, but is in fact compatible with any other religion.

NOTES

[1] In fact, in the discos of Amazonia, the more shrunken heads you have on your belt, the more women you pull. With the rest of us, it would be dollars.

[2] See, for example, the Tablets of the Law.

CHAPTER 8

Right Effort

Brothers, I know that your attention is imprisoned in the imaginary world of your thought.

Brothers, I know that looking inside yourselves requires an effort of will.

Brothers, make the effort to look inside yourselves.

Concentrate your attention on your thought, observe how it is born, grows and dies, how impermanent it is and how its fantasies are not real.

Brothers, by making the effort to look inside yourselves, you will free yourselves from the fantasies of your thought.

Then you will be able to turn your attention to the reality that surrounds you and it will be revealed to you in all its beauty and joy.

You will discover that in reality there is no suffering: suffering is only in your thought.

Brothers, make the Right Effort of concentrating your attention on your sensations, your emotions and your thoughts and you will achieve Right Concentration. [*Suttapitaka, Majjhima-Nikaya, Satipatthana Sutta*]

Summing up:

Right Effort consists of the will to implement Right Concentration; that is, the observation of our own thought.

The observation of our own thought does in fact require *an effort*. Why?

Because our attention is usually *magnetized* by our thoughts to such an extent that we *become our thoughts*.

When a thought crosses our consciousness (for example: 'I am a failure'), we assume that thought is real and we *become* that thought.

That is why we suffer.

Our Ego identifies with our thoughts.

It is *magnetized* by our thoughts.

This magnet is very powerful.

We really have to make *an effort* to escape it.

Habit, or rather *automatism*, keeps us prisoners of our thoughts, of our minds.

Coming out of our mind, becoming the observer of our own thought, implementing Right Concentration, is not in itself difficult to achieve: the difficult part is to *remember* to do so.

That is why the Buddha included Right Effort in the Noble Eightfold Path, as if it were a path in itself, side by side with the other seven.

But it is simply a preparation for the eighth element of the Noble Eightfold Path, the last and most important: Right Concentration.

CHAPTER 9

Right Mindfulness

You are intelligent children and I am certain that you can understand everything I tell you and put it into practice.

Children, when you eat a tangerine, you can eat it with awareness or distractedly.

What does it mean to eat a tangerine with awareness?

It means that when you are eating a tangerine, you know that you are eating it.

You enjoy its fragrance and sweetness to the full.

Children, what does it mean to eat a tangerine without awareness?

It means that when you are eating a tangerine, you do not know that you are eating it.

You do not enjoy its fragrance and sweetness.

In so doing, you cannot appreciate the splendid, precious nature of the tangerine.

If you are not aware of eating it, the tangerine is not real.

If the tangerine is not real, then whoever eats it is also not real.

That is what it means to eat a tangerine without awareness.

Children, to eat a tangerine with mental presence means to be truly in contact with reality.

Your mind does not chase after thoughts of yesterday or tomorrow, but dwells totally in the present moment.

Living with mental presence and awareness means living in the present moment, with a body and mind dwelling in the here and now. [Suttapitaka, Majjhima-Nikaya, Satipatthana Sutta]

Right Mindfulness, then, consists of *turning our attention to the reality around us, here and now, and interacting with it.*

Which is why it should more correctly be called **presence in reality**.

Right Mindfulness consists of **presence in reality**.

Presence in reality is fundamental to the achievement of buddha-ness, in so far as, not being focused obsessively on our own inner thoughts but on the outside world, on reality, it is an *unneurotic* psychological state.

It is therefore necessary to systematically turn our attention to reality.

And live in reality.

CHAPTER 10

Right Concentration

Brothers, practise Right Concentration.

Right Concentration is the noblest element of the Noble Eightfold Path.

Right Concentration consists of concentration on thought.

Concentration on thought consists of the detached observation of our own thoughts.

Observe your thoughts with detachment just as you would observe with detachment the distant flight of birds in the peace of the evening.

Learn from the earth: whether you strew it with sweet-smelling flowers or cover it with faeces, the earth receives each thing impartially, without preferences or aversions.

When a thought, whether pleasant or unpleasant, is born, do not let yourselves be trapped by it, do not become slaves to it.

Observe it with detachment and let it go: it will not grow inside you and will not produce the poisoned fruit of suffering.

If you let your thoughts grow, they become very powerful, take possession of you and make you their slaves.

Observing your thought with detachment, you will discover a great unsuspected truth: that your thought is not the product of your will but is an autonomous plant, independent of you, nourished by your attachment, and with its roots in your fear.

If you practise detached observation of thought, vain thoughts will cease and you will dwell in Pure Consciousness.

Detached consciousness of thought, if practised constantly, leads to Liberation.

Brothers, before learning to observe thought with detachment, you must learn to observe and calm your breathing, your body and your emotions.

When you have calmed your breathing, your body and your emotions, practise the detached observation of thought continuously.

Detached consciousness of thought, together with conscious observation of breathing, strengthens concentration.

With concentration, you will be able to see deeply into the nature of the five methods of perception: sensations, emotions, thoughts, will and consciousness. [Suttapitaka, Majjhima-Nikaya, Cularahulovada Sutta][1]

If by 'mind' we mean the totality of our thoughts, our emotions and our sensations, then we can define Right Concentration as the **detached observation of the mind**.[2]

Right Concentration consists of the **detached observation of the mind.**

NOTES

[1] This is a reference to the *Skandha*, the five means by which *perception* presents itself. For the sake of greater clarity, the terms used here differ from the traditional ones. To find out more, see Chôgyam Trungpa, *Glimpses of Abhidharma*, op. cit.

[2] It should be made clear that the term 'mind' does not indicate an *object* but an *act* or rather a set of acts; that is, a *process* or a *function*, specifically the function of *perception*, which Buddhist psychology subdivides into the five *Skandha*, as already mentioned.

CHAPTER 11

The essence of the Noble Eightfold Path

To sum up, looking at their *essence*, we can state the Noble Eightfold Path as follows.

1
RIGHT KNOWLEDGE
AWARENESS OF *CONSTANT CHANGE* AND THE *INTERDEPENDENCE* OF THINGS (ENLIGHTENMENT) AND THEREFORE *NON-ATTACHMENT*

2
RIGHT THOUGHT
ELIMINATION OF INVOLUNTARY NEGATIVE THOUGHT AND PRODUCTION OF VOLUNTARY POSITIVE THOUGHT

3
RIGHT SPEECH
(SECONDARY, IN SO FAR AS IT IS A MORAL RATHER THAN A PSYCHOLOGICAL PRECEPT)

4

RIGHT ACTION
(SECONDARY, IN SO FAR AS IT IS A MORAL RATHER THAN A PSYCHOLOGICAL PRECEPT)

5

RIGHT LIVELIHOOD
(SECONDARY, IN SO FAR AS IT IS A MORAL RATHER THAN A PSYCHOLOGICAL PRECEPT)

6

RIGHT EFFORT
WILL TO IMPLEMENT RIGHT CONCENTRATION
(SECONDARY, IN SO FAR AS IT IS IMPLICIT)

7

RIGHT MINDFULNESS
ATTENTION TO REALITY AND INTERACTION WITH IT

8

RIGHT CONCENTRATION
DETACHED OBSERVATION OF THE MIND

This, then, is essentially the original Buddhism, as taught by the Buddha.

As we see, it is a *psychological* rather than a religious discipline.

There is one important thing to say here.

You should not get too lost in theoretical discussions.

It is necessary to move to practice.

Buddhism is above all **practical**.

A Buddhist is someone who practises Buddhism, not someone who talks about it.

A person who devotes himself to theoretical discussions about Buddhism is not a Buddhist but a scholar of Buddhism.

As, according to tradition, the Buddha himself explicitly said in a famous passage:

Although my teaching is neither a dogma nor a doctrine, it is certain that some people take it as such. I must explain clearly that I teach a method for experiencing reality, and not reality itself, in the same way as a finger pointing at the moon is not the moon. An intelligent person will follow the direction indicated by the finger to see the moon, but anyone who sees only the finger and takes it for the moon will never see the real moon. I teach a method to be put into practice, not something to believe in or worship. My teaching can be compared to a raft that is used to cross a river. Only a fool would still cling to the raft once he has landed on the other bank, the bank of liberation.
[*Suttapitaka, Majjhima-Nikaya, Dighanakha Sutta*]

Buddhism has only one *practical* purpose: to eliminate suffering by achieving **buddha-ness**, which consists of a *permanent state* of **serenity**.

So now the question is: what to do *in practice* in order to achieve buddha-ness?

Undoubtedly, the Noble Eightfold Path constitutes the *protocol* to follow in order to achieve buddha-ness, but what does the application of this protocol lead to, *in practice*?

More precisely, what must we achieve?

That is, what should our *practical objectives* be?

It is necessary to be clear on this point, because hitting the target is only a matter of time: the important thing is to see it clearly in such a way as to know exactly in which direction to fire the arrows.

Let us therefore analyse the practical objectives of the Noble Eightfold Path.

This will be the theme of the next chapter.

CHAPTER 12

The practical objectives of the Noble Eightfold Path

It is important to understand the practical objectives of the Noble Eightfold Path because these are the objectives that lead us to *buddha-ness* and so they are the objectives we need to reach.

We have seen that the first element of the Noble Eightfold Path, Right Knowledge, consists of the *awareness of change and the interdependence of all things* and that this awareness constitutes *enlightenment*, which is the cornerstone of Buddhism, the foundation on which it is built.

From it we should then achieve *non-attachment*, which leads to liberation from suffering.

But the awareness of change and the interdependence of all things is a purely cognitive, that is, *intellectual*, objective. Non-attachment, on the other hand, is a *behavioural* objective.

Therefore it is distinct from the first, as far as reaching it goes.

In addition, non-attachment derives, strictly speaking, not from interdependence but from the awareness of *change*. Strictly speaking, therefore, the **first objective** is the *awareness of change*.

The first objective is the
AWARENESS OF CHANGE.

Non-attachment is the **second objective**.

The second objective is
NON-ATTACHMENT.

We have also seen that the second element in the Noble Eightfold Path, Right Thought, consists of the *elimination of involuntary negative thought* and the *construction of voluntary positive thought*, and the eighth element in the Noble Eightfold Path, Right Concentration, consists of the *detached observation of the mind*.

But both these actions in fact involve *control of the mind*.

Control of the mind is therefore the **third objective**.

The third objective is
CONTROL OF THE MIND.

We have seen that the third, fourth and fifth elements in the Noble Eightfold Path – Right Speech, Right Action and Right Livelihood – consist of *moral rules*, which, however important they are, do not constitute specific psychological powers to be acquired: in fact, we have defined them as *secondary*.

It is possible, therefore, to leave them out of account, in so far as they do not constitute *psychological* objectives to reach in order to achieve buddha-ness.

We have seen that the sixth element in the Noble Eightfold Path, Right Effort, consists of the *will to implement Right Concentration*.

Therefore it is not in itself a specific objective but simply the *will* to implement the third objective; that is, control of the mind.

We can therefore omit it from our objectives, since it is implicit in their pursuit.

Finally, we have seen that the seventh element in the Noble Eightfold Path, Right Mindfulness, consists of *presence in reality*; in other words, of turning our attention to reality and consciously interacting with it.

Presence in reality, then, is the **fourth objective** to achieve.

The fourth objective is
PRESENCE IN REALITY.

But there is another objective to reach, in order to truly achieve the state of buddha-ness: *universal love.*

The Buddha himself mentions *universal love* in relation to Right Thought, indicating how universal love is the mental dimension of the Buddha.

Brothers, Right Thought consists of thought in which there is universal love.

In reality, the love to which all creatures aspire is universal love.

In universal love there is compassion and devotion.

Compassion and devotion have as their aim the happiness of everyone and do not demand anything in return.

Without them, without universal love, life is without joy.

Through compassion and devotion to other people, through universal love, life is filled with peace and joy. [Suttapitaka, Majjhima-Nikaya, Piyajatika Sutta]

It is only through universal love that we can find *serenity*.

Universal love, then, is the **fifth objective** to achieve.

The fifth objective is
UNIVERSAL LOVE.

Ultimately, then, **the practical objectives of the Noble Eightfold Path are:**

1   **AWARENESS OF CHANGE**
2   **NON-ATTACHMENT**
3   **CONTROL OF THE MIND**
4   **PRESENCE IN REALITY**
5   **UNIVERSAL LOVE**

As each of us has the *potential* capacity to achieve these five objectives, we can say that these objectives are in fact five *powers*, which we simply have to implement.

As the Buddha said, they are already present inside us. We only need to *develop* them.

CHAPTER 13

A scientific method

Can the Buddha's original teaching be translated into a *scientific method*?

For a method to be classed as scientific, three things are necessary:

1 the *elements of the problem to be solved* must be known;
2 a *procedure* must be developed with which *to solve it*;
3 the practical application of this procedure should be within everyone's reach.

Let us first examine more closely the *elements of the problem* of how to become a buddha.

They are the *psychological conditions* that make it possible to achieve and maintain this state.

These psychological conditions are precisely the five *powers* we have identified in the Buddha's original teaching: *awareness of change, non-attachment, control of the mind, presence in reality* and *universal love*.

They constitute a *working protocol*.

For this protocol to constitute *a scientific procedure for solving the problem*, it is necessary for its applicability to follow a *criterion* of application.

In other words, the five powers should not be unconnected and independent of each other but instead present a *criterion* that makes it possible to pass from one to another.

In technical terms, a *consistency of application*.

Only in this way, in fact, can they constitute a *scientific procedure*.

But since these are psychological conditions, it is obvious that the consistency of application must be a *psychological consistency*.

It is necessary, in other words, that each of them is made possible, or even caused, by the one that precedes it on the level of psychological realization.

The five powers of the Buddha must therefore be examined in greater depth.

Let us begin with the first.

What does *awareness of change* derive from?

Obviously, from observation of reality.

But observation of reality can only be achieved through *presence in reality*.

Therefore presence in reality precedes awareness of change.

But presence in reality consists of turning our *attention to what is outside the mind,* and to do this we have first to free our minds of compulsive thought, which we can only achieve if we have taken *control* of it.

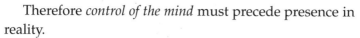

Therefore *control of the mind* must precede presence in reality.

And so we have this first sequence: 1: control of the mind; 2: presence in reality; 3: awareness of change.

But what does awareness of change lead to?

Obviously to non-attachment.

Non-attachment is therefore the fourth power.

And finally, non-attachment – precisely because it eliminates self-interest – spontaneously gives access to the fifth and greatest power of the Buddha, *universal love.*

Our project, then, becomes that of developing, in order:

THE FIVE POWERS OF THE BUDDHA

1   CONTROL OF THE MIND
2   PRESENCE IN REALITY
3   AWARENESS OF CHANGE
4   NON-ATTACHMENT
5   UNIVERSAL LOVE

This protocol, which essentially coincides with the Noble Eightfold Path and therefore with the Buddha's original teaching, presents the second required scientific condition: *consistency of application*, which in our case is a *psychological consistency* in so far as every power gives access, on the psychological level, to the following power.[1]

Now that we have identified the *procedure for solving the problem*, we still have to verify its *practical applicability.*

To do that, it is necessary to analyse in detail *how* we can develop these five powers.

Each of the following chapters is therefore devoted to one of the powers.

NOTE

[1] The psychological consistency of the *powers* corresponding to the Noble Eightfold Path is so obvious that it is impossible not to suspect that this may well have been the original order of the Noble Eightfold Path, as presented by the Buddha.

CHAPTER 14

Control of the mind

The first power that needs to be mastered, *control of the mind*, is very important: in fact, it is the basis of the whole process by which we may achieve the state of buddha-ness.

As we have seen, Buddha himself stated explicitly:

Right Concentration is the noblest element of the Noble Eightfold Path.

It therefore needs to be approached with particular care and *determination*: what Buddha called Right Effort.

Developing *control of the mind* requires, in fact, an *effort of will*. The other powers come more spontaneously once the first of them has been developed, but this first one takes a certain commitment.

Control of the mind is not a power invoked only by the Buddha.

All *initiates*, from Buddha to Plato, to Seneca, St Augustine, Pico della Mirandola, Muhammad, Meister

Eckhart and Sai Baba,[1] have seen it as a basis for spiritual evolution and advocated it.

To control the mind, Buddha asserts, it is necessary to *observe* it.

In other words, to observe our own sensations, our own emotions, our own thoughts.

Especially our own *thoughts*.

Because thought is the cause of emotion, and therefore the cause of suffering.

In fact, emotion has its origin in *thought*.

If I think about the loss of a loved one, an emotion is produced in me that I call 'suffering'.

If, on the other hand, I think about a loved one who is beside me, an emotion is produced in me that I call 'pleasure'.

In other words, it is thought that produces our *mental suffering*.

Now, the important thing to understand is that thought that produces suffering is *not voluntary*.

Thought that produces suffering is not voluntary.

In fact, no one deliberately produces suffering for himself, since that would go against the genetically programmed instinct for survival that we all share. (Masochists are no exception: the suffering they procure for themselves heals their sense of guilt and therefore ultimately gives them an elation of the Ego and therefore a pleasure.)

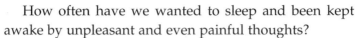

How often have we wanted to sleep and been kept awake by unpleasant and even painful thoughts?

How often have we tried not to think unpleasant thoughts and found we cannot do without them?

How often have we tried not to think about what we have lost, our failures, our disappointments, our mistakes, but to no avail?

How often have we tried not to think about our future, the challenges that await us, the risks we run, the circumstances of our death, and been unable to escape these thoughts?

We are incapable of avoiding thoughts that make us suffer!

Against our will!

But how is it that we produce this mental suffering, even if only involuntarily?

How is it that we produce involuntary thought?

Because it is *automatically* produced by our *memory* (our unconscious).

Involuntary thought is, in fact, merely a manifestation of the *tension* deriving from traumas (acts of violence, anxieties, fears, losses, failures, uncertainties) recorded in our *memory*. (Tension is actually *electrical tension* that remains in the neuronal circuits of the brain and produces thought as part of its natural process of discharge: if we suffer a trauma, the mental alteration that it produces remains in our mind for a long time after the trauma. In fact, we cannot stop thinking about it.)

87

The acts of violence, anxieties, fears, losses, failures and uncertainties we have experienced remain engraved in our memory and reappear in the form of *thoughts* that recall and reproduce those emotions.

The thing that it is essential to understand, the thing we must never forget, is that thought that causes us suffering is the *automatic product of the tension recorded in our memory.*

Thought that causes us suffering is the automatic product of tension recorded in our memory.

In the condition of *neurosis*, the thought that gives us suffering, also called *tensional* thought, constitutes almost the whole of our mental activity.

How can this be?

Because thoughts *reproduce.*[2]

Thoughts reproduce.

Thoughts are like seeds that produce plants.[3]

And negative thoughts produce *poisonous plants.*

These poisonous plants constitute our *suffering.*

Thought is the cause of our mental suffering and this is precisely what the Buddha discovered and defined.

Therefore, it is thought that we must learn to control.

Control of the mind consists of control of thought.

The Buddha devoted two elements of the Noble Eightfold Path to control of the mind: Right Thought and Right Concentration.

As we have seen, Right Thought consists of the elimination of *negative thoughts* and the construction of *positive thoughts*. (In accordance with Eastern tradition, we can define as *negative* all those thoughts that lead to *separation* [mistrust, suspicion, antipathy, resentment, hate, etc.] and as positive all those thoughts that lead to *union* [trust, acceptance, sympathy, benevolence, love, etc.].)

In addition, we have also seen that negative thoughts are *involuntary*.

It is obvious that the positive thoughts that we must introduce into our minds, on the other hand, are in fact *voluntary*.

The operation we have to do ultimately is to replace *involuntary negative thoughts* with *voluntary positive thoughts*.

Basically what we need to do is perform a kind of *mental hygiene.*

But which negative thoughts are replaced?

And with which positive thoughts?

According to tradition, the Buddha drew up a list of them, when he expounded the *Four Contemplations* and the *Four Incommensurables.* [cf. Chapter 6, Right Thought]

We can sum up the list as follows, taking into consideration the whole of the thought-emotion complex:

INVOLUNTARY NEGATIVE THOUGHT	VOLUNTARY POSITIVE THOUGHT
agitation	concentration on breathing
antipathy	kindness
cruelty	compassion
anger	love
hate	compassion
attachment	reflection on impermanence
lust	reflection on the end of all things

It needs to be said immediately that having recourse to the Four Contemplations and the Four Incommensurables proposed in Right Thought is a *last resort.*

It is done only in the case of *very strong suffering.*

That is, in a case in which negative thoughts *systematically* overwhelm your mind.

The *normal* practice of control of the mind is that which is expounded in Right Concentration.

That is, *detached observation of thought.*

As the Buddha said:

Observe your thoughts with detachment as you observe with detachment the distant flight of birds in the peace of the evening. [*Suttapitaka, Majjhima-Nikaya, Cularahulovada Sutta*]

The detached observation of thought neutralizes it: it takes away its emotional charge and thereby breaks the chain of its *self-reinforcement* in memory and consequently its force of reproduction.

How does this happen?

Through an act of *disidentification*.

There is in fact a *psychological law*:

We are dominated by everything with which we identify and we dominate everything with which we disidentify.[4]

When we are overwhelmed by thoughts that give us suffering, we normally take them to be *our own work*: we think we ourselves are the *authors* of those thoughts, we *identify* with them and take them to be *true*.

If, for example, there is in our mind the thought of a loss and a consequent emotion of fear, we usually identify with the author of that thought and with the person who is overwhelmed by fear.

The emotion of fear then becomes very strong. (It is as if the Ego, identifying with the thought and with the emotion that follows from it, yields to them its energy, which is what constitutes *our mental energy* and therefore our very *life energy*.)

This, in addition, causes that thought and that fear to imprint themselves deeply in our *memory* and to arise again insistently for a long time to come.

But that is *neurotic*, because we are not the willing authors of that thought: it is produced automatically by memory at the urging of the fear that has been recorded in it *in the past.*

As a result of the identification of our Ego with that thought and that fear, through the psychological law mentioned above, *we are dominated by it.* It is as if the Ego had its own force of gravity that flings it into the mind, in other words, into our thoughts, sensations and emotions, so that it forgets itself and loses itself in them.

To better understand this process of the *state of tension* or *identification with the tensional thought,* the diagram shown below may be useful.

Within the area of the *conscious mind*, our *Ego* identifies with the author of the *tensional thought*, although it is in fact a product of the *unconscious mind.*

State of tension or of identification with the tensional thought

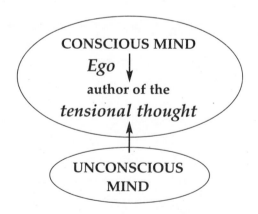

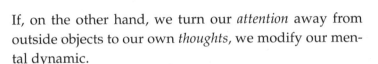

If, on the other hand, we turn our *attention* away from outside objects to our own *thoughts*, we modify our mental dynamic.

If we observe a specific thought and a specific fear in our mind, we become an *outside observer* who simply takes note of the presence of that thought and that fear.

In this way, that thought and that fear no longer concern our Ego, because our Ego has shifted from the object of that thought and that fear to the *outside observer*.

This cools down the fear, so to speak, and prevents it from being recorded in our memory, instead of strengthening that thought and favouring its reproduction in the future.

In this way the tensional thought, with its burden of suffering, is *neutralized*.

In scientific terms, our *centre of identification*, the Ego, with which we identify, shifts from the thought to the *observer*.

This function of our brain is known under the name *consciousness*.[5]

The observer is not the thought.

Therefore he or she is not involved in the tension that is present in the thought.

And since the Ego is the driving force behind the tensional energy that constitutes the emotion, this is reduced. (It is as if consciousness, which is the function with which the Ego can most fully be identified, were the natural seat of *mental energy*: until consciousness is immersed in the mind, so to speak, and we therefore identify with our thoughts and our emotions, these are manifested in all their strength and sweep us away: we become slaves of them. Consciousness gives thoughts and emotions all their energy.)

The process can be illustrated by the following diagram:

State of self-consciousness or of self-observation

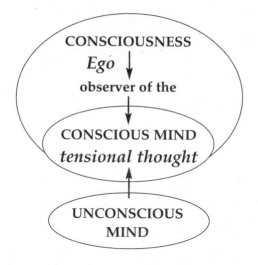

In the state of consciousness, the Ego becomes the observer of the *tensional thought* present in the conscious mind but produced by the unconscious mind.

The action of observing our own thought – consciousness – constitutes a genuine *specific cerebral function* peculiar to human beings, although it is activated spontaneously only in exceptional cases. (In particular, in the case of *serious accidents* [it is common in such cases to see your own life passing in front of you like a film]: you find you are looking at yourself from the outside, so to speak, and you see yourself acting as if you were someone else.)[6]

It is precisely through this cerebral function – consciousness – that we implement the observation of our thought.

Our Ego shifts from the author of our thoughts to an *impersonal observer.*

We may call him the *Noble Detached Observer.*

To implement self-observation of thought it is necessary to become the Noble Detached Observer.

It is actually the detached observation of thought that constitutes the *control of the mind* that we have seen to be essential not only to achieving presence in reality but also buddha-ness itself.

A buddha, in fact, is always aware of the automatism of his own thoughts and is always detached from them; he does not let himself be enslaved by them.

A buddha always observes his own thoughts with detachment and is always aware of their automatism.

What you must think, in order to develop this power, is that your mind is merely an *organ of your body*, which produces thought the way the gall bladder produces bile and the suprarenal glands produce adrenalin.

(I know that idealists will be shocked by this statement. Don't worry, I'm used to it. Unlike Schopenhauer, who answered the objection that his thought had nothing to do with reality with the words 'Too bad for reality!', I answer, 'Too bad for thought!')

The mind is an **organ of the body.**

And you can manipulate it, train it, strengthen it and command it as you wish, like any other organ, like the lungs or the bladder. (Yogis can also control the gall bladder and the suprarenal glands. With a bit of training you can do it, too. I'm already planning my next book, *How to control the gall bladder and the suprarenal glands in two weeks.* Be patient!)

The mind can be manipulated.

It is only a matter of *practice*.

And therefore of time.

If you have never done it, it may seem difficult to observe your thoughts.

But there are tricks.

The first is this: *try to stop thinking.*

Of course, you can't do it.

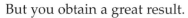

But you obtain a great result.

You look inside your mind.

After all, how can you find out whether or not your mind is carrying out your order to stop thinking if you don't look inside it?

That's the first stage.

A second stage is that of observing your mind, and therefore your thoughts, *using your senses.*

Look inside your mind using *your sight.*

Do you see images?

They are not thoughts, strictly speaking, but they are nevertheless an activity of the mind.

If you see them, you are looking inside your mind.

Now use *your hearing.*

You will hear a voice speaking.

It is your *thought.*

You've caught it!

Because, as I have already said, thought manifests itself in the form of *words.*

This final procedure is the most effective, the one you will be able to adopt normally.

Do not, however, become obsessed with the observation of thought, if you have difficulty in implementing it: the important thing is to become aware that *your thoughts are the products of your unconscious mind.*

This is the result of the observation of thought and is therefore substantially what control of thought consists of.

This is true especially of *negative thoughts.*

*When you have a negative thought you must
be aware that it is produced by your unconscious
mind.*

The awareness of the automatism of thought must be implemented *systematically*.

In a few days, if you apply yourself consistently, your negative thoughts will lose their force and you will find that you have a clearer mind – still crossed by automatic thoughts, because they never stop as long as you live, but deprived of their virulence, therefore less capable of disheartening and depressing you – in other words, of making you suffer.

The awareness of the automatism of thought is the *fundamental methodology* to implement in order to achieve *control of the mind*.

Tradition reports, however, that the Buddha said:

Brothers, before learning to observe thought with detachment, you must learn to observe and calm your breathing, your body and your emotions.

When you have calmed your breathing, your body and your emotions, practise the detached observation of thought consistently.

The detached awareness of thought, together with the conscious observation of breathing, reinforces concentration.
[*Suttapitaka, Majjhima-Nikaya, Cularahulovada Sutta*]

Why is that?

Because the mind is not a structure or a function separate from the body, which means that you cannot calm your mind without also calming your body.

Mind and body are in reality the same structure, which we could call *psychosoma*.[7]

As highlighted in *Vipassana*, the traditional Buddhist meditation technique, the functions that make up the human person are distinguishable, didactically, in three processes: *breathing, body* and *mind*.

These three processes are integrated and interact with each other, which is why any tension present in one of them corresponds to a tension present in the other two and each of them is both cause and effect of the others.

This diagram may make things clearer:

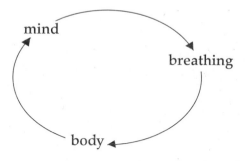

As can be seen from the diagram, each process has a relation with the others that is a relation of *conditioner* and *conditioned*.

Vipassana applies particularly to breathing.

In fact, its complete name is *Anapanavipassana*, which means 'full awareness of breathing'.[8]

Because breathing is the simplest process of the three and therefore the one that can most easily be kept under control.

The practice of concentration on breathing is very powerful.

Through it, according to the tradition, the Buddha attained *enlightenment*.

It is easy, by concentrating on breathing, to actually achieve *mental emptiness*.

When you have learned to practise an awareness of breathing and thought, you will easily attain mental emptiness.

Mental emptiness is the natural condition of the mind, just as rest is the natural condition of the body. [*Suttapitaka, Majjhima-Nikaya, Cularahulovada Sutta*]

Mental emptiness is very useful because it allows us to eliminate the tension – that is, the *suffering* – normally present in our minds.

A buddha is someone who basically lives in mental emptiness.

A buddha basically lives in mental emptiness.

Two things need to be said about this, however.

The first is that mental emptiness should not be pursued *obsessively*.

In fact, instead of eliminating *tension*, it would cause it.

The second is that mental emptiness cannot *always* be maintained.

Please don't get the wrong idea – that in order to become a buddha you have to stop thinking for good, which is not only impossible but actually dangerous.

Simply, thought should not be used pointlessly but only in cases where it is really needed, where it is useful to our *well-being* or even our very *survival*.

On the one hand, it is practically impossible to stop thinking for good, because involuntary thought is formed automatically. On the other hand, we need to think in order to solve *practical problems.*

This is, in fact, the biological function of thought: to solve practical problems through the simulation of their possible solutions.

The state of buddha-ness consists, more precisely, of a mental state in which thought is used *voluntarily* and is limited to the solution of practical problems. When it goes beyond this natural aim and is produced automatically due to a neurotic urge, it is *contained and attenuated*, because consciousness, the *Ego*, remains outside it in the position of the Noble Detached Observer.

Practising concentration on breathing does not require specific conditions either of time or of place.

You don't have to lock yourself in a silent, empty room or withdraw to a hermitage.

It can be practised at any time and in any situation, even while strap-hanging on a bus.

All you need to do is

take eight deep breaths and calm your breathing.

It is necessary, however, to learn how to use the whole of your lungs in order to breathe, and not just part of them.

If you like, and if possible, all you need is to keep your breathing calm for as long as you choose.

It is not important to keep it calm for a long time, but to calm it often.

Therefore, instead of long sessions of calm breathing, shorter but frequent sessions are advisable.

As frequent as you choose and you feel is good for you.

In conclusion, the *exercise* you must practise to achieve *control of the mind* is as follows:

EXERCISE 1

1 **I calm my breathing;**
2   **using my breathing I relax my body;**
3 **I continue to keep my breathing calm and I observe with detachment the thoughts and emotions that come into my mind;**
4 **I am aware that my thoughts are produced by my unconscious.**

This exercise is easy and leads you to *mental emptiness.*

EXERCISE 1A
(in case of overwhelming negative thoughts)

1   I become aware that my mind is being overwhelmed by a negative thought-emotion;
2   I develop in my mind the opposing positive thought-emotion.

Practise EXERCISE 1 *for a week.*
    If necessary, also practise EXERCISE 1A.
    You do not need specific conditions or surroundings.
    The exercise can be done anywhere.
    How many times and for how long?
    That's up to you.
    The more you do it, the sooner you will become a buddha and the more *permanently* you will become one.
    In this first week your principal objective will be:

to control your mind.

If you like, during this week you can use a supporting *mantra*, to be recited *mentally*, as and when you choose.

    (A *mantra* is any constantly repeated word or phrase. A prayer, for example, is a mantra. The use of a mantra is important. It has an influence on the *unconscious*. It records a *suggestion* in the unconscious that automatically produces thoughts, emotions and patterns of behaviour. In other words, it *transforms* you. In addition, it has two other outcomes. It prevents the automatic production of negative thoughts. It gives you total control of your mind [and of your body, if you recite it in conjunction with your breathing]. Two rules: always recite it *mentally* and don't tell anyone about it. The first rule stops you being taken to a mental home against your will. The second stops you dispersing the energy of your transformation.)

Try the following:

I control	*breathe in*
my mind	*breathe out*
I am	*breathe in*
a buddha	*breathe out*

NOTES

[1] A contemporary, considered in India an *Avatar*, an incarnation of the divinity (*Ganesha*), has followers all over the world: 'It is necessary to control and eliminate the conflicts of desires afflicting the mind, which should be focused in a single direction.' [Sathya Sai Baba, *Prema Dhyana*.]

[2] The sedimentation of thoughts in memory comes with all their *stock of emotions*: therefore, when a thought generates an emotion the two are recorded together and it is precisely that emotion that recalls the thought. The stronger the emotion, the more frequently the thought to which it relates is reproduced.

[3] In the yogic tradition, thought is in fact defined as 'seed' (*bija*), because it produces other thoughts: cf. Patañjali, *Yoga Sutra*, I, 46 and I, 51.

[4] R. Assagioli, *Psychosynthesis. A Manual of Principles and Techniques*, 1965.

[5] Consciousness has been a major subject of interest of the *Christian religion* for centuries: according to Catholic theology, it is precisely the activation of consciousness that gives rise to *free will*, which is capable of implementing our *humanity* and revealing our *divine origin*. In modern times, *psychology* has also taken an interest in consciousness (e.g. R.M. Bucke, P.D. Ouspensky, W. Hall, A.H. Maslow and especially R. Assagioli). Contemporary *neuroscience* has investigated consciousness as a cerebral function. We cannot help but be amazed when we consider that consciousness is practically a brain that watches itself functioning.

[6] 'In situations of danger (for example in war or at certain moments during mountaineering) there comes a strengthening of consciousness, a state of "superconsciousness" in which normally impossibile actions and heroic acts are performed.' [R. Assagioli, *Psychosynthesis. A Manual of Principles and Techniques*, op. cit.]

[7] See K. Dychtwald, *Bodymind*, 1977.

[8] For more on the theory of *Anapanavipassana*, see Buddhadâsa, *Mindfulness with Breathing*, 1988. I don't, however, advise you to apply it in its traditional version, which is too long and complicated.

CHAPTER 15

Presence in reality

It is not possible to develop this power, the second in our project to become a buddha, if your mind is overwhelmed by thoughts.

We see therefore how the previous power, control of the mind, which leads to the *attenuation of thought*, is necessary to the development of this second power.[1]

Not only that, but it makes its development possible and easier.

Once thought has been attenuated, or the mind actually emptied, you will in fact be able to turn your attention spontaneously to reality.

But what is reality?

Reality is the environment that surrounds us.

Reality is the environment that surrounds us.

In fact, for each of us, the environment that surrounds us is *our reality*.

This isn't such a trivial fact.

Let me set you a test.

We are in New York, sitting on the terrace of the Times Square Brewery.

I ask you, 'Do you think the Place Pigalle in Paris is real?'

You probably answer, 'Yes.'

But it isn't.

If you are in New York, in Times Square, the environment that surrounds you is Times Square in New York, not the Place Pigalle in Paris.

Therefore *your reality* is Times Square in New York.

Paris and the Place Pigalle are not the environment that surrounds you.

They aren't your reality.

They are only in your mind, in your memory, not in your *reality*.

Herald Square in New York isn't real to you either, if you are in Times Square.

Because Herald Square isn't the environment that surrounds you. Herald Square isn't real to you.

Do you understand what I'm saying?

Your reality is the environment that surrounds you and that you perceive with your senses.

In other words, your reality is Times Square in New York.

Nothing else.

Paris and the Place Pigalle may be the reality of someone in Paris, in the Place Pigalle, but they are not *your* reality.

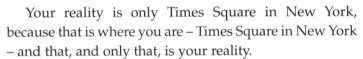

Your reality is only Times Square in New York, because that is where you are – Times Square in New York – and that, and only that, is your reality.

If you behaved in Times Square in New York as if you were in the Place Pigalle in Paris, you would not be in tune with reality.[2]

You would not be present in your reality.

Don't tell me.

You're going to say, 'But what about war?'

Of course war is real, but it is real for those who are in it, not for us who are sitting here, calmly reading this book.

If you phone soldiers at war, they will confirm it to you immediately and even ask you to break open your piggy bank.

Because for us, sitting here calmly reading this book, the war is only in our mind, not in our reality.

There are two worlds:

1   *the world of the mind*
2   *the world of reality.*

In simplified terms

The world of reality is real, the world of the mind isn't real.

Of the objects that present themselves to our consciousness, in fact, some belong to the reality that surrounds us, while others belong to our mind – that is, to *our memory*.

We tend to believe that both kinds of objects are real, but that is not the case.

Only the objects that belong to the environment that surrounds us are real, not those that belong to our memory.

You may think this is a debatable point, if you are still strongly anchored to the world of your mind, but I will give you incontrovertible proof.

A relative of yours who has died is undoubtedly still present in your memory, but it is obvious that he is not present in the environment that surrounds you (or even in the environment that doesn't surround you), which means that he is not real.

Unfortunately.

Other examples that are less dramatic but just as incontrovertible can be found in our daily experience.

One example will suffice.

One day, the great Neapolitan actor Totò arrives late for an appointment.

His friend asks him, 'What happened to you?'

'I'm late because someone stopped me and said, "Vincenzo, you bastard!"'

'What did you say?'

'Nothing. I kept quiet.'

'What happened then?'

'Then he went on, "Vincenzo, you son of a bitch!"'

'And what did you do?'

'Nothing. I kept quiet.'

'And did he carry on?'

'Oh, yes. He went even further. "Vincenzo," he said, "I'm going to kill you!"'

'And what did you do?'

'I went away.'

'What? Didn't you react?'

'No.'

'Why not?'

'Why should I care? I'm not Vincenzo!'

This distinction between words, thought and reality in Naples, where there are many buddhas, is quite clear. (To be a buddha in Naples isn't optional as it is in other places: it's compulsory, if you want to survive.)

The further north you go, the more this distinction fades.

In Sweden if you call someone an idiot, he commits suicide.

The attribution of reality to the objects of our mind is the *technical cause* of our mental suffering.

We suffer because of the fantasies in our mind.

The fantasies of your thought are not real.

They are generated by your attachment, and therefore by your desire, your hate, your anger, your fear.

Brothers, the fantasies of your thought are generated by you yourselves. [*Suttapitaka, Majjhima-Nikaya, Satipatthana Sutta*]

We suffer because we take the fantasies of our mind *for reality.*

111

It is fundamental, therefore, that you learn to distinguish between reality and the fantasies of your mind.

A buddha is always aware of this distinction.

The state of buddha-ness includes an awareness of the distinction between the world of the mind and the world of reality.

This **awareness** has to become **permanent**.

It is this that leads us to abandon the world of the mind and enter the world of reality.

Brothers, deprive your imaginary fantasies of your approval and they will vanish. [*Suttapitaka, Majjhima-Nikaya, Satipatthana Sutta*]

I know you can advance the objection that is advanced, with good reason, by all those who are not only fond of the world of their own minds but exhalt the beauty and power of its creations.

Achieving the second power of buddha-ness, presence in reality, does not negate either that beauty or that power, but simply offers you a way out of your *suffering*, which is generated by your own mind.

Buddhism has this one essential purpose: liberation from suffering.

All it is saying is: you cannot defeat the fantasies in your mind if you stay within your mind.

You have to come out of your mind and enter reality.

That is why attenuating thought allows us, quite naturally and without any effort – in other words, spontaneously – to implement the second power of buddha-ness: *presence in reality.*

In reality there is never suffering.

I know that this is another truth that is difficult for you to believe.

Let us again take an extreme case.

You have just lost a loved one.

You think that reality is the cause of your suffering, because in reality the person you have lost is no longer there.

But that is precisely the point.

In reality that person is no longer there, but that's all.

In reality there is no suffering.

The sun continues to rise, the clouds continue to race across the sky and the birds continue to sing.

The suffering is only inside you.

You think that reality is the cause of your suffering and therefore you attribute your suffering to reality itself.

But suffering is not an object that can be found in reality.

It is a *mental state.*

In other words, it is inside your *mind.*

A famous *Zen koan* says:

Show me the hand in which you are holding your suffering.

You can't do it, because suffering belongs to the *world of the mind* and not the world of reality.

In fact, the same reality causes suffering to some, but not to others.

(After a month's meditation, the disciple to whom the master put the *koan* quoted above went back to the master and said, 'The right hand,' and the master beat him on the back with a stick [Zen masters are very aggressive]. After another month the disciple came back, with a triumphant air, and said, 'The left hand,' and the master again hit him on the back with a stick. At this point the disciple cried, 'Damn you, you senile old man, you and your stupid questions!' [literal translation from the Japanese]. The master embraced him joyfully and said, 'At last you've understood, my son, that they're stupid questions!')

Presence in reality is the *Zen experience.*

That is why the Zen experience cannot be described in words but only *experienced*, as all those who write books about it state quite frankly. In which case, you may wonder, why do they write books about it?[3]

Precisely because the Zen experience is the experience of presence in reality.

We can then draw on the Zen tradition to give an idea of such an experience.

It reports the following anecdote.

As Yao-shan Wei-yen was quietly sitting cross-legged, a monk came to him and asked:

'What are you thinking in that motionless position?'
'I am thinking of that which is beyond thought.'
'How do you go about thinking of that which is beyond thought?'
'By not thinking.' [Hui-Neng (Wei-Lang), *Sutra*, 23]

But you don't have to go to China or Japan to meet Zen practitioners.[4]

You just have to go to Sardinia.

One day in Orgòsolo I met a shepherd.

I asked him, 'What do you do all day?'

'I watch the sheep.'

'And what do you think about?'

'What should I think about? I make sure no one steals the sheep!'

Presence in reality has no need for further explanations, because it is not a question of intellectual knowledge but of *experience*.

To fully understand it, do one thing.

Put this book down and go to the bathroom.

Get in the shower or the bath and turn on the tap.

And think, 'I'm taking a shower. It's a perfectly normal thing to do.'

When you have become aware that taking a shower fully clothed is not at all normal, you will have made contact with reality and you will have grasped the difference between reality and thought.

The exercise you must practise to achieve *presence in reality* is as follows:

EXERCISE 2

1 I calm my breathing, I relax my body, I observe my thoughts with detachment;
2 I come out of my mind and I observe the environment around me;
3 I perform common actions (interactions with reality).

For example, dust the piano and put a coaster under the coffee cup. If you don't have a piano or even a coaster, but above all if you don't have a cup of coffee, you're really in trouble.

4   I remain in reality.

In other words, keep dusting. When you've finished, start cleaning the windows. Then hoover the carpets. And finally turn over the mattresses and make the beds. If you do this exercise every morning, you can do without the cleaning lady.

Practise this exercise *for a week* (after which you can rehire the cleaning lady).

You do not need specific conditions or surroundings.

This exercise can be practised everywhere (even in other people's houses – in this case you may also gain something).

As often and for as long as you like.

But the more you do it, the better it will be (the more you do it, the more you gain).

In this second week your principal objective will be:

to live in reality.

If you like, during this week you can use a *supporting mantra*, to be recited *mentally*, as and when you choose:

I am living	*breathe in*
in reality	*breathe out*
I am	*breathe in*
a buddha	*breathe out*

NOTES

[1] *Zen* also aims at attenuating thought in order to then concentrate attention exclusively on reality: in fact, the one purpose of the *koan* (an absurd puzzle that the master sets the disciple) is to convince the follower of the pointlessness of thought and persuade him to turn his attention to reality.

[2] And you would probably end up spending the night in a police station: Americans, as we know, are puritans. The Place Pigalle is full of sex clubs and if you behaved in the clubs in Times Square as you might behave in the clubs of the Place Pigalle (for example, touching the backsides of the girls) you would end up in a police station; Americans are very sensitive when it comes to the backsides of their girls.

[3] Have you ever wondered how people who practise Zen earn a living (since Zen consists of doing absolutely nothing)? Writing books! I am a Zen master!

[4] Zen did not originate in Japan, but in China in the 6th century AD, where it went under the name *Chan* (an alliteration of the Sanskrit *Dhyan*, contemplation, a phase of yoga). It was then exported to Japan in the 13th century, where it took the name *Zen*.

CHAPTER 16

Awareness of change or enlightenment

Having acquired the second power, presence in reality, it is possible to develop the third power of buddha-ness, *awareness of change.*

Because it is presence in reality that allows us to observe reality objectively and discover that there are no objects, events or people in it that always stay the same.

Even inside us, in our mind, our mental states do not stay the same. In fact

everything is in a state of constant transformation.

This is the *great discovery* we make when we observe reality for what it is.

This great discovery also constitutes the famous **enlightenment**.

Along with it comes another discovery: that all things in the universe are *interdependent.*

119

Imagine a huge billiard table upon which an infinite number of balls are constantly moving and hitting each other: the movements of each one of them are determined by the movements of *all the others*.

The universe is exactly the same.

It is this interdependence that gives rise to constant change: no one ball can stop because the movements of all the others force it to move constantly.

In the same way, there are no people, things or situations that stay the same.

The *physical sciences* tell us the same thing.

This cognitive acquisition is undoubtedly an *intellectual act*.

And it is relatively easy for anyone to do.

Then what?

Are we all enlightened?

Is enlightenment so simple and easy to obtain?

Is that all there is?

Of course not.

An enlightened person is not only someone who has discovered that everything in reality is subject to constant change, but someone who, once he has reached this awareness, *never loses it*.

Enlightenment consists of the constant *awareness* that reality is always changing.

In fact, for enlightenment to be permanent, this discovery has to be introjected at a deep mental level – in other words, at an *unconscious level* – and that cannot happen simply by thinking it.

It must be acquired through an act that also comprises an *emotional state*, since the unconscious mind (that is, *memory*) remembers in a way that favours reproduction – in other words, in a way that conditions conscious perception, only those experiences that are accompanied by an emotional state.

That is the reason why the Buddha says it is necessary to have *personal experience* of this acquisition or awareness.

We have to observe reality and experience personally the fact that it is in a state of constant transformation and therefore devoid of any permanence.

Loss, for instance, becomes an opportunity for this experience.

It is a way of using suffering as a means to encourage the growth of consciousness, as the Buddha himself indicated.

This experience then becomes a discovery charged with *emotion*, because it demolishes our belief that reality is made up of things, people and objects that we think are fixed and always the same, as if outside time, eternal, *never fading*.

Only in this way can such an experience become for us, as it was for the Buddha, an *enlightenment*.

For that to happen, it is necessary to remember *as often as possible*, through the observation of reality inside us (intra-psychic) and outside us (extra-psychic), *the awareness of its constant change*.

Loss thus becomes a subject on which we must often meditate.[1]

But why does a representation of reality form in our mind which makes us believe that there exist things that are fixed, definite, always the same over time?

Reality (and life) is like a film, consisting of the action resulting from images projected one after the other, not of single images.

Life is a film, not a still photograph.

Life is *dynamic*, not static.

But what we do is take an image from the film, file it away in our memory, and attribute a real existence to it.

That is how we see our mothers, our fathers, our friends, ourselves.

As still photographs, fixed and determined.

And we believe that they are determined, fixed, always the same.

Indeed, we expect that they will always be the same and we are surprised and angry when we discover this is not the case, that they change and are not what we thought they were.[2]

Life is a film, but in our minds there are photographs and we take those photographs for life.

Why?

Because our *child personality*, which always takes us backwards, which is ready to come to the fore at every existential crisis (an illness, a loss, a failure), and which some do not overcome and never abandon, is incapable of dealing with change because it is incapable of dominating reality.

So we create for ourselves an illusion of certainty, cutting out images from the film of our life and attributing reality to them.[3]

That is why experiencing Buddhist enlightenment also means *growing psychologically*, moving from the child personality to the adult personality and becoming capable of facing the uncertainty inherent in the constant transformation of reality.

> **Enlightenment includes a psychological growth from a child personality to an adult personality.**

The *exercise* you must practise in order to achieve *enlightenment* is as follows:

EXERCISE 3

1 **I calm my breathing, I relax my body, I observe my thoughts with detachment;**
2 **I observe the environment around me;**
3 **I observe the constant change inside me and outside me;**
4 **I am aware of the precariousness of all things.**

Practise this exercise *for a week*.

You do not need specific conditions or surroundings.
It can be practised everywhere.
As and when you choose.
In this third week your principal objective will be:

to see change .

If you like, during this week you can use a *supporting mantra*, to be recited *mentally*, as and when you choose:

I see	*breathe in*
change	*breathe out*
I am	*breathe in*
a buddha	*breathe out*

NOTES

[1] Meditating on death is a leitmotiv of Buddhism, but please don't think this marks it out as tragic or pessimistic. On the contrary, the thought of death enhances the importance and sacredness of life, making us appreciate and enjoy it more. The ancient Romans kept a symbolic skeleton at their feasts to remind them of the transience of life ('Memento mori!') so that they could enjoy themselves even more.
[2] This cognitive error leads to enormous suffering: married couples very often part because one of the two spouses discovers (maybe after twenty years) that the other person is not 'the way he (or more frequently she) thought'.
[3] Which constitutes a genuine *neurosis*.

CHAPTER 17

Non-attachment

The discovery that reality is constantly changing has one major *consequence*.

We become aware that

there is nothing fixed to which we can become attached.

And that is how the fourth power of buddha-ness – *non-attachment* – develops spontaneously in us.

Acquiring the fourth power, *non-attachment*, is the most difficult step to take in our path towards buddha-ness.

But it is also the most important.

Because it represents a permanent transition from the child personality to the adult personality.

It means abandoning totally and permanently the *need for protection*, for *points of reference*, for *certainty*.

There is no certainty in the real world.

The real world is in a constant state of *change*.

Therefore there are no points of reference, and there are no certainties.

Reality sometimes shows this fact to us in the most brutal fashion – for example, when we lose a loved one.

We are then forced to see reality as it is and for a moment, even if it is only through our pain, we experience *enlightenment*.

But a moment later, in self-defence, we fall back on the illusion of permanence, stasis, certainty.

It is our *attachment* that gives us the illusion that there are points of reference and certainties.

Therefore, if we let go of attachment, we can abandon certainties.

Is that such a terrible thing?

Thinking of it from the outside – in other words, from outside non-attachment and inside the condition of attachment, dependence, illusory certainty – yes, it is truly terrible, because we feel alone and abandoned.

Having no points of reference in our life, no certainties, is indeed terrible.

But only to someone who cannot do without points of reference and certainties, who needs help and protection.

In other words, a *child*.

Not an adult.

The adult has gained the ability to look after himself without needing help or protection.

He does not need anyone.

Therefore he does not need points of reference or certainties.

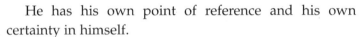

He has his own point of reference and his own certainty in himself.

He can do without anyone or anything.

Because he is *focused on himself.*

That is why he is capable of going further and becoming a *parent.*

He is so sure of himself, so capable of helping himself that he also becomes capable of *helping others.*

He becomes capable of being a parent.

Because non-attachment also makes him overcome the *personal selfishness* of the adult.

He demands nothing more of other people, he expects nothing more from other people.

In fact,

a buddha has no expectations: he accepts and enjoys what is there.[1]

Expectations are the principal cause of our suffering.

We can see, therefore, that achieving the state of buddha-ness also means developing our adult and parent personalities.

The teaching of the Buddha involves the whole of our *psychological evolution.*

In the natural evolution from child to adult to parent, the development of these three natural personalities is necessary to the development of the fourth personality, that of the buddha.

The buddha personality, the state of buddha-ness, is in fact impossible to achieve if we have not first developed our adult and parent personalities.

Following the method set out in this manual, which is the teaching of the Buddha himself, you will become, if you are not already, an adult and a parent, and then at last a *buddha*.

Non-attachment is a *crucial* power for this evolutionary process.

One thing, however, needs to be clarified.

Non-attachment does not mean non-love.

Non-attachment does not mean *I don't care about you, you don't matter to me.*

Non-attachment is not indifference.

Non-attachment is *non-demand for possession.*

Non-attachment is *non-demand for possession.*

Because attachment is not attachment to the other person but to yourself.

It is *attachment to the Ego.*

As we shall see, the result of non-attachment is love, whereas the result of attachment is selfishness.[2]

But how can we free ourselves of attachment?

We have dozens, hundreds, of attachments.

Large and small.

What can we do to free ourselves of them?

The first thing to do is *become aware of them.*

Become aware of your own attachments.

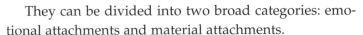

They can be divided into two broad categories: emotional attachments and material attachments.

Despite the clarification above, it would be better to call emotional attachments by the name *emotional possessions*, otherwise you will have difficulty understanding what follows.

You can free yourself of *emotional* possessions by considering their *precariousness*.

Or rather, the precariousness of the presence of that person in your life.

This is the great driving force behind non-attachment, which makes it possible to develop this very great power: awareness of the precariousness of each and every thing.

Awareness of the precariousness of each and every thing makes it possible for you to develop the power of **non-attachment.**

You must meditate *frequently* on the precariousness of each and every thing.

You must *always* be aware of the precariousness of each and every thing.

You must meditate **frequently** *on the* **precariousness of each and every thing.**

You must **always** *be aware of the* **precariousness of each and every thing.**

It is the systematic use of the power that you have acquired – the power of the *awareness of change* – that will allow you to develop this power, the power of *non-attachment*.

Become aware of the precariousness of existence and therefore of the precariousness of the presence in your life of the people who are the objects of your emotional attachment.

They are not eternal.

They won't be there for ever.

They won't even be there all your life.

Therefore you cannot demand their presence.

As we have seen, to demand the presence of someone does not mean to love them.

It means to *want to be loved by him or her.*

Behind this false love there is in fact a *need* and therefore a demand.

But need is not pleasure, it is suffering, in so far as there is a constant risk that it will not be satisfied.

The philosophy of the Buddha is *pleasure*, not suffering: it was against suffering that he fought.

That is why he preaches love.

Because love is joy and pleasure.

To love is to enjoy the other person's existence, independently of his or her presence.

Could it be that the love of God is like that?

I am not telling you to abandon the people you love.

I am only asking you to become *free* to enjoy the people you love when they are there and to enjoy something else when they are not there.

To become free of demands towards them and capable of enjoying your availability to them.

Because being available, giving yourself, is a pleasure.

This is love which, as you see, derives from non-attachment, or rather from non-possession.

You can free yourself of *material* attachments by considering your *ability to do without them.*

Begin by identifying your small attachments.

Don't start with *vices* like smoking, drinking and so on.

These are not small attachments: they are among the biggest you have.

Because they are *teats.*

The teats a child needs.

And your child personality, not having a mother's teats to suck, sucks on cigarettes, chocolates, whisky and so on.

For the moment let them be.

You will be able to free yourself of them only when your adult personality has gained the upper hand.

Take a small attachment, such as watching your favourite TV show.

And start to think how your life would be if this programme were cancelled.

You realize that nothing particularly tragic would happen.

You would simply do without it.

That's all.

Which is exactly what will in fact happen sooner or later.

Sooner or later they'll stop making the show.

Of course, you don't have to stop watching it.

A buddha isn't a masochist.

You simply have to become capable of doing without it.

You have to become capable of seeing it or not seeing it, as you wish.

In other words, to become *free* to see it or not see it.

This is the elimination of material attachments.

As an exercise, don't watch it sometimes, and do something else interesting instead.

Then move on to another small attachment and so on until you have gone through all your attachments and can even tackle and destroy the big ones I mentioned above, like cigarettes, chocolates and so on.

When you have freed yourself of your attachments, especially your attachment to the demand that everything always stays the same and just the way you like it, you will discover a wonderful thing.

That an awareness of the precariousness of life and of all things makes you appreciate their uniqueness and their beauty a thousand times more than you did before.

Every moment will become unique and unrepeatable and you will become aware of that.

And then you will savour each and every thing, each and every person, each and every situation with incredible pleasure, however tiresome or obnoxious they are.

What's more, and this is the greatness of buddha-ness, you will no longer even see the tiresome, the obnoxious, the bad, the ugly.

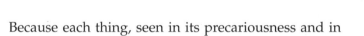

Because each thing, seen in its precariousness and in its uniqueness, is wonderful, simply by existing.

Not to mention people.

Every person in fact, however petty, mediocre, even tiresome, antipathetic, wicked, and above all stupid, is unique and wonderful in so far as he exists, and is alive and real.[3]

And if you have freed yourself of attachments, you will be able to appreciate and love that person.

You will be able to enjoy him when he is there.

Without demanding that he be there when he isn't.

And without demanding that he should be different from how he is.

That is, without *attachment*.

Because attachment is always attachment to what is not there, in so far as it is *desire for what is not there.*

Attachment is desire for what is not there.

Non-attachment, on the other hand, is basically non-desire: *not demanding what is not there is but appreciating and enjoying what is there.*

Non-attachment is not demanding what is not there but appreciating and enjoying what is there.

Try to make this leap and your life will change.

Make the great leap, renounce every certainty and become aware at every moment of your life of the

absolute precariousness but at the same time the uniqueness, the unrepeatability, the wonder, the miraculousness
of each and every moment, each and every thing with
which you come into contact, each and every person,
each and every situation.

Develop the fourth power, non-attachment, and your
buddha-ness will truly be within your grasp.

The *exercise* you must practise to achieve *non-attachment*
is as follows:

EXERCISE 4

1   **I calm my breathing, I relax my body, I observe my
thoughts with detachment;**
2   **I observe the environment around me;**
3   **I am aware of the precariousness of each and every
thing;**
4   **I let non-attachment grow inside me.**

Practise this exercise *for a week.*

You do not need specific conditions or surroundings.
It can be practised everywhere.

In this fourth week your principal objective will be:

to free yourself of attachments.

If you like, during this week you can use a *supporting
mantra*, to be recited *mentally*, as and when you choose:

I have no	*breathe in*
attachments	*breathe out*
I am	*breathe in*
a buddha	*breathe out*

NOTES

[1] That is why the Buddha is traditionally called *tathata*: that which is.

[2] How many people, claiming they love us, demand from us presence, availability, loyalty, dedication, sacrifice, things that in reality are suffering for us and pleasure for them? True love is the desire for the other person's happiness, not ours.

[3] Stupid people are a remarkable invention. First of all, if they didn't exist, we wouldn't be able to feel intelligent. Secondly, they are very amusing. The best way to amuse yourself is to be sure they are stupid. It takes guts to suspect they might be intelligent. You might discover that you're the stupid one.

CHAPTER 18

Universal love

If you stopped after acquiring the four preceding powers, you would not yet be a buddha.

You would be a self-focused, self-sufficient individual capable of enjoying every situation, but basically isolated from other people, deprived of that capacity for communication with other living creatures and with the whole universe that makes us self-aware human beings capable of *loving*.

You would have developed your *adult* personality, you would have learned to face the precariousness and uncertainty of life alone.

You would also have developed your *parent* personality, which makes you capable of accepting other people as they are and appreciating their beauty and uniqueness.

And maybe of helping them.

But you would not be a buddha.

Because you would not have achieved that *serenity* that, as we have seen, is the fundamental characteristic of a buddha.

And that can only be achieved through *universal love*.

Only through universal love can life be filled with peace and joy. [*Suttapitaka, Majjhima-Nikaya, Piyajatika Sutta*]

The state of buddha-ness cannot therefore be achieved fully until this fifth power – *universal love* – has been developed.

In fact, it is the *essence* of the state of buddha-ness.

Only through *universal love* can we achieve that **serenity** that we set as our original *objective*.

Why then, you may ask, strive to develop the four preceding powers and not aim immediately to develop universal love?[1]

Because universal love cannot be developed if the four preceding powers have not been developed first.

We cannot love the whole universe if we have not first learned to control the mind, to be present in reality, to see change and to let go of attachments.

Universal love can only be nourished with a mind free of fear, in contact with reality, and liberated from selfish needs.

They are impediments, limits, negative conditions.

Universal love has no limits, no conditions.

Universal love is an emotion that fills our mind and our body to our last cell.

Universal love means expanding ourselves to the whole universe, acquiring consciousness of the universe to which we belong, *becoming the universe.*

Universal love means being in contact with the universe, becoming the whole universe.

What would you think of a drop in the ocean that, as it hovered in the air above the ocean, thought that it existed as a being separate from the ocean to which it belonged?

That it was mad![2]

But that's exactly what you do every time you feel alone, every time you feel you are separate from other people, and from the universe to which you belong.

That is what the Buddha discovered with *enlightenment*: that we are merely cells of an eternal, infinite universe in a state of constant transformation.

And this same thing has been experienced by mystics throughout history and in every culture: they have experienced an awareness of belonging, of communion with the whole, which they have identified with a divinity.

But how to develop universal love within yourself?

The Buddha gave us a great pointer.

Compassion.

In universal love there is compassion and devotion.

Compassion and devotion have the happiness of all as their aim and do not demand anything in return. [Suttapitaka, Majjhima-Nikaya, Piyajatika Sutta]

Compassion is *the plant from which the flower of love blooms.*

139

Only compassion makes love grow inside us.

Why do we naturally feel love for babies?

And not only human babies, but the babies of any animal.[3]

Because babies, in their weakness, their helplessness, their inability to feed themselves, defend themselves, survive, *arouse our compassion.*

But what does compassion mean?

Literally it means feeling the same 'passion'; that is, the same suffering.[4]

In other words, making other people's suffering ours.

Understanding other people's suffering.

It is *understanding* that makes compassion possible.

According to tradition, Siddhartha himself

saw that understanding and love are one and the same: without understanding there can be no love.[5]

Understanding means *knowledge.*

Knowledge of the past, the life, the suffering of the other person.

That is why we feel compassion for our spouses and our friends.

Because we know their past, their life, their suffering.

If you are interested in the past, the life, the suffering of the other person, you cannot help but feel compassion for his suffering.

And feeling compassion for his suffering means *becoming him.*

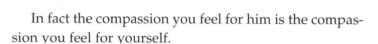

In fact the compassion you feel for him is the compassion you feel for yourself.

It is with yourself, therefore, that your journey towards universal love begins.

You know your own past, your own life.

You know your own sufferings.

How could you not feel compassion for your own sufferings?

It is not a question of self-pity, of feeling like a victim, but genuine compassion for the sufferings of the child, the youth, the man or woman that you have been, that you are.

If you are capable of compassion, acceptance, forgiveness and respect for the child, the youth, the man or woman that you have been, that you are, you are capable of love for yourself.

And learning to love yourself is the first step towards learning to love other people.[6]

When you have learnt to accept yourself, to forgive yourself, to have compassion for your own sufferings, your own illusions, your own passions, your own dreams, your own disappointments, your own defeats, your own wounds, you will have learnt to love yourself.

And you will be able to love others.

Because you will then see in others the same sufferings, illusions, passions, dreams, disappointments, defeats and wounds.

This is what love really is: seeing ourselves in others.

It is that same act from which we started.

Identifying with the universe around us.

And then you become every living creature and cannot help feeling the suffering that afflicts every living creature.

In fact there is no substantial difference between us and other living creatures: we all share the fact that we belong to the universe, we are all involved in the experience of *suffering*.

Considering the suffering of all living creatures leads to *compassion* for all beings and compassion is nothing other than *love*.

If you have truly overcome your attachment to your next of kin, your relatives, your friends, to those few living creatures on whom you make your happiness depend, then you are free to love every living creature in the universe.

When we talk about love, we usually mean the love between parents and children, husband and wife, relatives and friends. Depending by nature on the concepts of 'I' and 'mine', this love is imprisoned in attachment and discrimination. People want to love only their own parents, their own spouses, their own children and grandchildren, their own relatives and friends. Since they are ensnared in attachment, they fear the ills to which their loved ones are exposed and worry even before they have happened. Then, when adversity comes, the suffering is terrible. Love based on discrimination causes prejudice; that is, indifference and even hostility towards those we exclude from our love. Attachment and discrimination are causes of suffering for ourselves and others. In reality, the love to which all beings aspire is universal love. [*Suttapitaka, Majjhima-Nikaya, Piyajatika Sutta*]

Because, as you can now understand, your attachment to those few living creatures wasn't true love.

It was the *need* to be loved by them.

True love, precisely because there is no attachment in it, does not carry any need with it.

You expect nothing from those you love.

It doesn't matter if they are aware or not of your love.

It doesn't matter if they are grateful to you or not.

It doesn't matter if they return your love or not.

Does it matter to a mother if her child is or isn't aware of her love?

Does a mother love her newborn baby any the less because it is not aware of her love?

Does it matter to a mother if her child is or isn't grateful for her love?

How many mothers continue to love their own children even when they are not at all grateful for their love?

Does it matter to a mother if her child returns her love or not?

How many mothers continue to love their own children even when they do not return their love?

And how many mothers continue to love their own children even when they steal, lie, cheat or kill?

That's what love is: *unconditional acceptance.*

This unconditional acceptance is the flower born of a plant with two roots: non-attachment and compassion.

See, then, how non-attachment allows you to develop universal love and how compassion allows you to nourish it and make it grow inside you.

Cultivate within yourself non-attachment and compassion and the flower of universal love will bloom spontaneously within you, just as a flower blooms spontaneously on the plant that generates it.

Universal love, like every other feeling, is in fact developed through *repeatedly experiencing it.*

It is through the repeated experience of love for a person that our love for that person is consolidated, becomes dominant over every other thing, becomes *absolute.*

In the same way, your love for the universe, for every being in the universe, which is none other than love for yourself extended to the whole universe, can be developed by experiencing it *repeatedly.*

In order to develop universal love within yourself, therefore, you must apply yourself to entering *on a daily basis* into communication with the universe and with the creatures in the universe, with their suffering, until you feel compassion for all creatures in the universe, until you reach an awareness that you are basically one with them.

Developing universal love means developing the *fourth personality* of which we human beings are capable.

It means going beyond our natural animality, going beyond our three natural personalities: child, adult and parent.

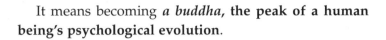

It means becoming *a buddha*, **the peak of a human being's psychological evolution**.

A buddha is the peak of a human being's psychological evolution.

The *exercise* you must practise in order to develop *universal love* inside you is as follows:

EXERCISE 5

1   **I am aware of belonging to the universe;**
2   **I consider the suffering of all beings;**
3   **I feel compassion for all beings;**
4   **I let my love for all beings grow.**

Practise this exercise *for a week.*

Even for this exercise, you do not need specific conditions or surroundings.

It can be practised anywhere, at a time of your choosing.

In this fifth week your principal objective will be:

to make contact with the universe and develop love for all beings.

If you like, during this week you can use a *supporting mantra*, to be recited *in your head*, as and when you choose:

I am	*breathe in*
a buddha	*breathe out*
I am	*breathe in*
love	*breathe out*

NOTES

[1] This eagerness to have it all and have it at once is typical of children. Do you want to test yourself? If you are eager to have it all and have it at once, you are a child.

[2] Calling a poor drop of water mad demonstrates that to become a buddha you really do go beyond all limits.

[3] There are people who raise crocodiles and are moved when they see the little crocodiles hatch and skip around, ready to snap at anything they see.

[4] The Latin word *passio* in fact means suffering: the passion of Christ is his calvary.

[5] *Buddhacarita*, III, 24.

[6] Jesus said 'Love your neighbour as yourself' [Matthew, 19: 19.]

CHAPTER 19

Maintaining the state of buddha-ness

Now you are a *buddha,* even though your buddha-ness is only at an *initial* stage and must be strengthened and amplified until it becomes *your true nature.*

Already at the end of this fifth week, in fact, if you have practised consistently, your buddha-ness has become a reality, as I promised you, and you can feel it inside you.

Once you have achieved buddha-ness, you nevertheless have to let it take root until it becomes *permanent.*

What is now necessary, therefore, is to help the state of buddha-ness *take root,* although it will no longer be a commitment as it has been during these five heroic weeks, but a *pleasure* that can be renewed every day.

It consists simply of practising *the final exercise once a day.*

FINAL EXERCISE

1 I calm my breathing, I relax my body, I observe my thoughts with detachment;
2 I observe the environment around me;

3 I am aware of the precariousness of each thing;
4 I free myself of every attachment;
5 I let my love for all beings grow.

This exercise coincides basically with *Vipassana*, the traditional Buddhist meditation.[1]

And it puts you in contact with your five powers.

The five powers of the Buddha.

With practice, it will only take you a few minutes.

After a time, which varies from person to person, you will feel that you can do without even this exercise of meditation and your state of buddha-ness will have become your true nature.

You will then have become a true buddha.

For this to happen you first need to understand a few things.

The first thing to understand is that you must put your serenity *above any other thing*.

Your serenity has to be placed above any other thing.

Do not think of this as a selfish attitude.

You cannot solve any problem better with anxiety and fear than you can with calm and serenity.

You cannot help anyone, if you do not preserve your serenity.

It's like when a plane is full and the oxygen masks descend from the overhead compartments.

You can't help your children to put on their oxygen masks if you don't put one on yourself first.

You cannot help other people if you feel sick.

Serenity in fact means *effectiveness*.

Being close to a serene person gives serenity and pleasure.

Therefore, if you have serenity inside you your mere presence gives serenity to other people and helps them.

And this is an act of *love*.

The second thing you have to understand is that suffering has *three immediate causes*, which all derive from attachment: *expectations, fears* and *guilt feelings*.

Suffering has three immediate causes: expectations, fears and guilt feelings.

But all three are *unfounded*.

Expectations are a demand that reality is as we want it to be, and it is obvious that this cannot happen in any systematic way.

It is not the fault of other people if our expectations meet with disappointment.

We simply need to stop having them.

Fears are always fear of something that is not there.

If a bus is about to hit me and I feel fear, that's the right reaction.

It's the only way I can save myself.

But if I am sitting in my armchair and I feel fear at the thought that if I go out I might get hit by a bus, that is a fear of something that isn't there.

It's an *imaginary fear.*

And imaginary fears are unfounded: they are *neurotic.*

Guilt feelings are absolutely lacking in foundation.

Guilt exists only if you do evil knowing that it is evil and with the specific intention of doing it.

But only a madman can do something like that.

A normal person *never* does it.

So when you blame others for your own suffering, you are making a fundamental error.

As I said at the beginning of this manual, it isn't other people who create your suffering, but your reaction to their actions.

If your husband or wife runs off with someone else, it's natural for you to blame him or her for your suffering.

But if you think carefully about it, you discover that not only do you have some responsibility for your spouse's running off (no one runs away from a wonderful person) but also that your suffering is absolutely *selfish* and therefore exclusively your problem.

You are certainly not suffering because your spouse is unhappy, because he or she isn't, but because you are unhappy.

And why are you unhappy?

Because you miss him or her.

But what are you really missing?

Obviously, his or her presence.

In other words, your *possession*.

But if you have developed non-attachment, which actually means non-possession, your suffering loses its reason for being.

And if you have also developed love, then you cannot help rejoicing at the happiness that he or she has found with someone else.

It means that you were not made for each other.

Now that you are a buddha, you have realized that your suffering does not depend on other people's behaviour but on your own expectations, your own fears, your own guilt feelings.

And it is the same for them.

Rather be aware of one thing: suffering is *necessary* to grow in awareness.

Could it even be that it was your suffering that led you to read this book and undertake your own path to buddha-ness?

That is why suffering must be respected.

Respecting the suffering of every person as his opportunity to grow in awareness: that is the Buddha's attitude.[2]

Wanting to take away other people's suffering at all costs or taking the burden of other people's suffering on yourself is *neurotic*.

Think first of taking away your *own* suffering.

Only then can you think of taking away other people's suffering.

But only if they ask for help.

Do not become a slave to the boy scout complex, which forces you to escort an old lady across the road even when that old lady doesn't want to cross the road.

If someone asks for help, give it.

Indeed, devote your life to helping those who ask for help.

That is the *practice* of universal love, which is sterile if it remains in the realm of contemplation.

But give them your help if they ask for it, not because you think they need it.

Let them say what they need, don't tell them what they need.

Those who bend over backwards to give other people what they think is good for them are not exponents of universal love but of emotional and cultural colonialism.

And that's why they feel they are such good people.

They always say, 'I've received much more than I've given.'

And it's true.

If you have liked using mantras and want to keep doing it, you can use the following *mantra* for as long as you like:

I am   *breathe in*
a buddha   *breathe out*[3]

NOTES

[1] It is, however, a simplified and much more easily practicable version of the traditional *Vipassana*, which has sixteen phases [cf. Buddhadâsa, *Mindfulness with Breathing*, op. cit.]

[2] In accordance with Eastern culture, in which every living creature follows his own destiny determined by his actions (*karma*).

[3] This mantra can be used for a lifetime. It is very powerful.

Envoi

You have now set in motion the wheel of your *karma*.

It will bring your *spiritual evolution* to fruition.

It is not mere chance that you have read this book and followed its instructions.

Many others have seen it and have not even considered it.

Many others have read it and forgotten it.

You have followed it because you were ready to follow it.

It has simply brought your *spiritual evolution* to fruition.

Because there was in you a *seed* of that buddha-ness and that universal love, which you are now preparing to let grow inside you until they fill your heart and your life, until they finally give your life a meaning, a purpose, a direction in the general economy of the universe.

Because becoming a buddha, fighting to become one and remain one, gives meaning and purpose to life.

Few people manage it.

You are one of those few.

That is why this book was written: to bring to fruition your evolution and that of those who, like you, are ready.

To become a buddha.

On your way towards buddha-ness, you have
beside you with their power and their energy all
the buddhas who have preceded you.
Their strength is yours
their awareness is yours
their love is yours.